INSTRUCTOR'S MANUAL

Regimes,
Movements,
and Ideologies

INSTRUCTOR'S MANUAL

Second Edition

Regimes, Movements, and Ideologies

A Comparative Introduction to Political Science

Mark N. Hagopian

Longman
New York & London

INSTRUCTOR'S MANUAL
Regimes, Movements, and Ideologies, Second Edition

Longman Inc., 1560 Broadway, New York, N.Y. 10036
Associated companies, branches, and representatives
throughout the world.

Copyright © 1984 by Longman Inc.

Developmental Editor: Irving E. Rockwood
Editorial and Production Supervisor: Ferne Y. Kawahara
Manufacturing Supervisor: Marion Hess
Composition: Media Presentation

ISBN   0-582-28467-8

Manufactured in the United States of America

CONTENTS

The second edition of <u>Regimes, Movements, and Ideologies</u> incorporates a number of improvements intended to lower the book's level of abstraction without sacrificing the book's distinctive approach. Thus I have retained the tripartite focus on regimes, movements, and ideologies but have deleted some conceptual treatments that are more properly the concern of advanced political science majors. Perhaps this validates the maxim that sometimes "less is more." But perhaps more significant is what has been brought into the text. The new edition, I think, is something between a wholly new book and a simple cosmetic update. I have retained what I felt were strong aspects of the first edition. The text remains strongly conceptual, because this is the ultimate form of knowledge in a truly comparative political science. However, I have tried in almost every chapter to incorporate more case-study materials to illustrate, amplify, or qualify concepts and typologies. This, naturally, is the type of material the beginning student can most readily ingest and digest.

These more concrete portions of the text are either biographical in nature or show how a particular notion displays itself in the politics of a given country. In the first instance, for example, there are brief biographies of people like FDR, de Gaulle, Idi Amin, Mussolini, Hitler, Stalin, and Reverend Jim Jones. Indeed, with some of these figures the treatment is faintly "psychohistorical," an approach that I favor more than some of my colleagues. At any rate such a stylistic modulation of the book's strongly conceptual bent should go over better with the students than some of the first edition's typologies.

In the case studies, properly speaking, I have tried to give examples of various concepts from different countries. For example, Fascist Italy illustrates the single-party in an authoritarian regime; Stalin's USSR and Nazi Germany illustrate totalitarianism; Khomeini's Iran shows the differences between revolt and revolution; France and Italy illustrate varieties of corporatism; and the Netherlands and Lebanon exemplify the notion of consociational democracy; and so on.

The second edition is also somewhat shorter in total pages, which is helpful in itself but also allows for supplementary readings. There are various avenues of approach here. One is to use only the text, which may be appropriate in certain teaching contexts. For the traditionally inclined, it might be wise to go in depth on certain countries. There are still plenty of specific treatments of the major countries available. These are either in single books or the traditional four-governments approach. Using the latter, however, will make very high reading and financial demands on students.

A third option is for the instructor to assign readings on topics that he has some special interest in or feels is treated inadequately in the text itself. The reservation here is the difficulty of the proposed supplementary book. Nonetheless, topics like revolution, nationalism, political parties, dictatorship, and European integration could be included.

Perhaps the most feasible area for supplementary readings is with the "isms," narrowly speaking. The text covers these in two fairly concise chapters so that there is room for a booklength treatment of ideologies along traditional lines. There are serviceable books here by Macridis, Ebenstein, Sargent, Cohen, and so on. A variation on this theme would be an anthology of primary source materials. Finally, there are monographs on most isms.

<u>Sequence</u>: In the first edition I felt that the three parts of the text

could be used in virtually any order. Now, I strongly recommend setting out with the regimes portion of the text, following then either with the movements portion or the ideologies portion. Quite possibly, the second best alternative is to start with ideologies, then go to regimes and conclude with movements.

Two Final Points: One is the inclusion of a Glossary-Index in the text. Given the amount of concepts and the range of the case studies, this should be far more useful to students than the usual subject and name indexes. Students should be encouraged to resort to the Glossary-Index. The second point is that the Instructor's Manual contains well over three times as many test items as the first edition. Each chapter has a minimum of sixty-five such items divided among multiple-choice, completion (fill-in), and true-false questions.

Part I: REGIMES

Chapter 1: Who Rules in the Modern State?

This chapter represents a condensed version of chapter 6 in the first edition.
It now serves as the introduction because of the importance of the question
"who rules." This is a question that most political scientists have firm
conclusions about and the material is not necessarily easy going for the
beginning student. It might be wise to let the students get their feet wet
with some or all of chapters 2-5 and then come back to 1.

If background research on this most central question of politics is
desirable, the seven works mentioned in the annotated Suggestions for Further
Reading at the end of the chapter are an excellent point of departure. Also
helpful are C. Wright Mills's The Power Elite and Robert E. Putnam's The
Comparative Study of Political Elites (Englewood Cliffs, N.J.: Prentice-Hall,
1976).

1. Vilfredo Pareto is most associated with the term
   *A. governing elite   D. interest group
    B. bourgeoisie   E. charisma
    C. power elite

2. In elite theory, rapid, wholesale "circulation" of the elite is
    A. reform   *D. revolution
    B. change   E. equilibrium
    C. stagnation

3. In addition to wealth, birth, and military prowess as the base of his "ruling class," Gaetano Mosca refers to
    A. land   *D. knowledge
    B. charisma   E. technology
    C. religion

4. What does Mosca call the system of ideas that helped to justify the rule of the ruling class?
    A. ideology   D. charisma
    IB. political formula   E. divine right
    C. legitimacy

5. What tendency does Mosca oppose to the democratic tendency in human societies?
    A. liberal   *D. aristocratic
    B. oligarchic   E. antidemocratic
    C. polyarchic

6. According to James Burnham, the separation of what two things has resulted in the "managerial revolution"?
    A. superstructure/substructure *D. ownership/control
    B. economics/politics   E. services/manufacturing
    C. Marx/Engels

7. The three components of C. Wright Mills's "power elite" are the warlords, the corporate rich, and
    A. the mass society   D. the politicians
    B. middle levels of power   *E. political directorate
    C. nongoverning elite

8. What is the pluralists' acid test for determining the existence of a ruling elite?
    A. income distribution   D. social background
   *B. studying decisions   E. political influence
    C. the political formula

9. What do critics of the pluralist model charge that it neglects?
    A. nondecisions   D. access
    B. interest groups   E. the public interest
   *C. public policy

10. Some pluralists suggest that current interpretations of Soviet politics are often unduly influenced by
    A. Marxism
    B. the elitist concept
    *C. the totalitarian model
    D. Weberian sociology
    E. Neo-Marxism

11. What do Neo-Marxists consider political elitism to be?
    *A. bourgeois ideology
    B. political formula
    C. substructure
    D. profit maximization
    E. the managerial revolution

12. For Neo-Marxists, which group encompasses professionals, small businessmen, small farmers and artisans, and white collar workers?
    A. the proletariat
    B. the ruling class
    C. the working class
    *D. the petty bourgeoisie
    E. the masses

13. What do Neo-Marxists call the most privileged and hence conservative members of the working class?
    A. apparatchiki
    B. mass society
    C. bourgeoisie
    D. nongoverning elite
    *E. labor aristocracy

14. Whom do Neo-Marxists see as the chief "conscious or unconscious allies of existing economic and social elites"?
    A. the bourgeoisie
    *B. top civil servants
    C. the warlords
    D. trade unions
    E. the superrich

15. Which of the following provided a "Neo-Marxist" analysis of communist regimes?
    *A. Milovan Djilas
    B. Ralph Miliband
    C. Friedrich Engels
    D. Robert Dahl
    E. C. Wright Mills

16. Which of the following is a Weberian "status group"?
    *A. an Indian caste
    B. AFL-CIO
    C. American power elite
    D. a ruling class
    E. the bourgeoisie

17. What did Max Weber consider the key to class affiliation?
    A. race
    B. birth
    *C. market position
    D. power
    E. status

18. What is it called when a lower group resents the privileges and arrogance of a higher group?
    A. class struggle
    B. revolution
    C. circulation of elites
    D. reaction formation
    *E. status resentment

19. What does a "mixed political elite" mix?
    A. elites and nonelites
    *B. classes and status groups
    C. racial groups
    D. aristocrats and oligarchs
    E. the three estates

20. For Weber what is the polar opposite of rational-legal domination?
    A. traditional
    B. legitimate
    *C. charismatic
    D. political
    E. ideal

21. In Leninist language, "kulak" means
    A. peasant
    B. middle peasant
    C. poor peasant
    D. rural proletarian
    *E. rich peasant

22. Which of the following best reflects Karl Marx's view of the peasantry?
    A. reformist
    B. critical
    C. revolutionary
    *D. reactionary
    E. rebellious

23. In some ways modern intellectuals are the counterpart to premodern
    *A. priests and prophets
    B. monarchs
    C. aristocrats
    D. tribal chieftans
    E. slaves

24. Undivided sovereignty characterizes which form of modern state?
    A. federation
    B. Greek polis
    C. confederation
    *D. unitary state
    E. government

25. Which of the following distinguishes federations from most confederations?
    A. states
    *B. no right of secession
    C. prefects
    D. United Nations representation
    E. satraps

Completion Questions

1. Pareto's, as with most stratification models, can be depicted in the form of a PYRAMID.

2. Pareto once remarked that history was the GRAVEYARD of aristocracies.

3. Gaetano Mosca called his ruling minority the ruling or POLITICAL class.

4. Mosca's two types of political formula are the rational and the RELIGIOUS.

5. The variable number of social FORCES makes the later Mosca's theory more pluralistic.

6. According to James Burnham, Stalinism, Nazism, and New Dealism all represent MANAGERIAL ideologies.

7. Thinkers who see highly-trained specialists in control of economy and polity call this new form of rule TECHNOCRACY.

8. C. Wright Mills relegated most elected officials and interest group leaders to the MIDDLE levels of power.

9. Critics say that elite theory involves the three C's of consciousness, coherence, and CONSPIRACY.

10. Robert Dahl objects that elite theorists mistakenly endow their alleged ruling elite with both potential for control and potential for UNITY.

11. The pluralist view of the power structure can be depicted as a sort of headless PYRAMID.

12. As in American baseball or football, pluralists sometimes describe the role of government as that of an UMPIRE.

13. According to the Neo-Marxist T. B. Bottomore top MANAGERS are not really "independent of the upper class of property owners."

14. Another name for the big bourgeoisie is the class of CAPITALISTS.

15. Neo-Marxists consider IDEOLOGY more a vague and diffuse view of things than an explicit, programmatic set of guidelines.

16. Milovan Djilas found that the emergence of a new CLASS marked the transition from revolutionary to dogmatic communicsm.

17. Pluralism focuses on social differentiation, while Neo-Marxism and elitism lay greater stress on social STRATIFICATION.

18. Most defenses of the inequality of status groups involve an ORGANIC conception of society.

19. Charisma is originally a term taken from RELIGION.

20. In contrast to the pure capitalist, the peasant does not produce solely for the MARKET.

21. Groups that have been politically mobilized because their livelihood, social status, or scheme of values is endangered are called CRISIS strata.

22. True middle-peasants who own their land and work it are known as independent SMALL-HOLDERS.

23. According to Lewis Feuer, extremist political ideologies have a special attraction for INTELLECTUALS.

24. Proponents of federalism stress experimentation, participation, size of territory, and FREEDOM as its outstanding virtues.

25. Certain critics of political elitism believe that its essence lies in anti-<u>MARXISM</u>.

True-False Questions

1. Elitism and Neo-Marxism seem to have more in common in their views of the power structure than either has with pluralism. (T)

2. Mosca's political formula is closer to the Neo-Marxist view of ideology than it is to Weber's three modes of domination. (F)

3. James Burnham's theory of managerial revolution can be considered a synthesis of Marxism and pluralism. (F)

4. In Burnham's estimation ownership of the means of production is ultimately the crucial factor in the power structure. (F)

5. Pluralism focuses on the interest group as the main political actor. (T)

6. The pluralist sees very strong vertical links between interest group leaders and the rank-and-file of organizations. (T)

7. The pluralist argues that the monolithic public interest should prevail over all lesser or sectional interests. (F)

8. In the Neo-Marxist view, desire for power unites owners and managers of industry. (F)

9. Neo-Marxists contend that a rising standard of living makes all talk of exploitation of the workers irrelevant. (F)

10. Leon Trotsky maintained that despite bureaucracy the Soviet regime remained a "workers' state." (T)

11. To all intents and purposes the distinction between classes and status groups can be safely ignored. (F)

12. Max Weber's notion of "rule by notables" suggests an elite that mixes individuals from both classes and status groups. (T)

13. The petty bourgeoisie is probably the most passive social group in a modern society. (F)

14. Those who oppose all attempts to decentralize Soviet power to the union-republic level are called "national deviationists." (F)

15. Pluralists are more optimistic about the democratic quality of most western countries than are the elitists or Neo-Marxists. (T)

This chapter has several basic concerns. It first tries to explore the notion
of constitutionalism, stressing how legalism limits both the substance and
procedure of governmental action. Keynote ideas are constitutional
dictatorship, separation of powers, and judicial review. Under
constitutionalism the following subtopics stand out: (a) the nature of
constitutional government--see especially C.H. McIlwain, Constitutionalism:
Ancient and Modern (Ithaca: Cornell University Press, 1961); M.J.C. Vile,
Constitutionalism and the Separation of Power (Oxford: Clarendon Press,
1969); and Carl J. Friedrich, Constitutional Government and Democracy
(Waltham, Mass.: Ginn-Blaisdell, 1968); (b) constitutional dictatorship--see
Clinton Rossiter, Constitutional Dictatorship (New York: Harcourt, Brace &
World, 1963); (c) on the comparative aspect of judicial review, see Taylor
Cole, "Three Constitutional Courts," reprinted in the 3rd ed. of Roy C.
Macridis and Bernard E. Brown, eds., Comparative Politics: Notes and Readings
(Homewood, Ill.: Dorsey Press, 1968).

The second basic concern is a thorough survey of parliamentarism, both in
its classic and its transformed versions. The underlying theme here is how
parliamentary regimes nowadays do not operate as our classic or "textbook"
account would have it. The balance has shifted away from parliament and
toward the government.

Technical points such as no-confidence and censure may be highlighted in
class. The theme of opposition has received increased attention in the past
decade or so: see Dahl's collection in Suggestions; Otto Kirchheimer's essay
"The Waning of Oppositions in Parliamentary Regimes," reprinted in Comparative
Political Parties, A.J. Milnor, ed. (New York: Thomas Y. Crowell, 1969).
Back issues of the journal Government and Opposition contain many useful
studies.

Also worthy of class attention is the whole problem of the causes and
effects of the "decline" of parliaments: see G. Loewenberg, ed., Modern
Parliaments: Decline or Change? (New York: Aldine-Atherton, 1971). The
essays by Bracher and Grosser in The New Europe, S. Graubard, ed. (Boston:
Houghton Mifflin, 1964) are relevant to this theme. Also helpful here is
A. H. Birch, Representative and Responsible Government (Toronto: University
of Toronto Press, 1969) for a view of the evolution of parliament in the
British context.

The third basic concern of this chapter is to explore presidentialism,
which is done through a look at American and French presidentialism. Some
underlying themes are the institutional weakness of the former despite the
"imperial presidency" rhetoric and the dependence of the impressive power of
the latter on pro-presidential majorities in the National Assembly. Here the
biographies of FDR and de Gaulle complement the legal-institutional
perspective with the personality variable.

At this point some discussion of the comparative merits of parliamentarism
and presidentialism seems warranted. Of the countless books on the American
presidency the classics by Corwin, Rossiter, and Burns as well as the recent
treatment by Cronin (see Suggestions) can be consulted with profit. The
Barber book on "presidential character" is a must for those who like the
personality emphasis.

1. Which term is closest to the classic Greek understanding of constitution?
    *A. political regime   D. judicial review
    B. written document   E. public policy
    C. democracy

2. Which of the following is a convention of the British constitution?
    A. party conclaves   D. orders-in-council
    *B. the vote of confidence   E. the Reform Act of 1832
    C. the monarchy

3. Which two types of limitations operate in consitutional government?
    A. written and unwritten   C. rights and duties
    B. interpretations and   D. state- and nation-building
        amplifications   *E. substantive and procedural

4. Beyond defining the institutional balance and citizenship, what have some recent constitutions included?
    *A. social rights   D. constitutional dictatorship
    B. checks-and-balances   E. separation of powers
    C. judicial review

5. Which of the following did not characterize the Roman dictatorship?
    A. limited duration   *D. the title of Caesar
    B. later liability   E. return to normalcy
    C. crisis situation

6. Modern constitutional dictatorship necessarily involves
    A. judicial supervision   D. martial law
    B. separation of powers   *E. strengthening the executive
    C. six months duration

7. The United States Supreme Court cannot
    A. overrule state courts   D. contradict the president
    B. refuse to hear appeals   E. reach split decisions
    *C. issue advisory opinions

8. Some countries have a Council of State which functions as a
    A. senate   D. cabinet
    *B. highest administrative court E. electoral college
    C. constitutional tribunal

9. Which doctrine impedes the full development of judicial review in certain countries?
    *A. parliamentary sovereignty D. checks-and-balances
    B. separation of powers   E. federalism
    C. Roman law

10. Which of the following could not be the title of the head of government in a parliamentary system?

A. prime minister
*B. president
C. chancellor

D. president of council of
ministers
E. premier

11. Which of the following is not part of the classic parliamentary model?
A. government by assembly
B. vote of confidence
C. collegial cabinet
D. the strong M.P.
*E. separation of powers

12. An attempt by M.P.'s to oust the government without the latter's agreeing
to the vote is called a
A. coup d'etat
B. vote of good faith
C. blocked vote
*D. vote of censure
E. vote of cessation

13. "Crisis" in the context of classic parliamentarism means
A. vote of censure
B. emergency decrees
C. disagreement between two houses of parliament
D. resignation of the prime minister
*E. lack of a pro-government majority

14. The major factor explaining the relative weakness of M.P.'s in modern as
opposed to classic parliamentarism is
A. decline of parliaments
*B. increased party discipline
C. constitutional dictatorship
D. unicameralism
E. quasi-presidentialism

15. In addition to lacking strong staff assistance, the British Prime
Minister, in contrast to the American president, faces a more powerful
A. parliament
B. supreme court
*C. cabinet
D. head of state
E. ministry

16. Which of the following is not among the principles for the existence of
upper houses?
A. hereditary nobility
*B. virtual representation
C. federalism
D. functional representation
E. indirect election

17. The basic official rules of parliamentary assemblies are often called
A. Robert's Rules of Order
*B. standing orders
C. conventions
D. folkways
E. lex naturalis

18. In contrast to the American Speaker, the Speaker of the British House of
Commons is
A. appointed rather than elected
B. Leader of the House
C. secretary-general
*D. a politically impartial figure
E. unable to guide debate

19. Standing parliamentary committees do not

A. survive from one election to the next
B. deal with definite subject matter
C. reflect the partisan complexion of the chamber
D. make law in Italy
*E. iron out differences between the two houses' bills

20. The general meeting of a party's M.P.'s is called the
   A. steering committee   D. annual meeting
   B. 1922 committee   E. select committee
   *C. caucus

21. When parliament acts as a watchdog against administrative misdeeds,
    it is called
    A. parliamentary sovereignty   *D. oversight
    B. statutory instruments   E. the rubber stamp
    C. responsible government

22. Both standing and select committees can be used for
    *A. investigatory purposes   D. replacing the cabinet
    B. direct passage of legislation   E. the filibuster
    C. bringing down governments

23. Which two roles of the American president do not find mention in the
    Constitution?
    A. commander-in-chief and chief executive
    B. chief executive and party chieftain
    *C. manager of prosperity and party chieftain
    D. chief diplomat and commander-in-chief
    E. chief executive and chief legislator

24. The "critical constituency" of the American president embraces
    *A. media, clergy, and intellectuals
    B. the federal bureaucracy
    C. the electoral college
    D. the Supreme Court
    E. business, labor, and farmers

25. Historians usually characterize James D. Barber's active-positive
    presidents as
    A. Democrats   D. strict constructionists
    B. conservatives   E. rigid and suspicious
    *C. strong

26. The presidency of Franklin Delano Roosevelt was characterized by
    A. an attack on the capitalist system
    B. weak leadership
    *C. cautious experimentation
    D. an active-negative leader
    E. reassertion of Congress

27. Franklin Delano Roosevelt's leadership evokes Machiavelli's contrast
    between the "lion" and the "fox" because he
    A. always felt that the ends justify the means
    B. believed in the supremacy of foreign policy

12

       *C.   combined force with cunning
        D.   could combine prudence with principle
        E.   synthesized left-wing and right-wing ideas

28. One difference between French and American presidentalism is that
        A.   the French leader is indirectly elected
        B.   the French president must resign after a nonconfidence vote
       *C.   the French president must have countersignatures for certain acts
        D.   the French president is basically a figurehead
        E.   the French president is neither chief executive nor chief legislator

29. Former President Charles de Gaulle of France
        A.   was the president of the Fourth as well as the first one of the
             Fifth Republic
       *B.   resigned after an adverse vote on a referendum
        C.   was defeated in his bid for reelection
        D.   resigned after the parliament ousted his premier
        E.   was a member of the Socialist party

30. De Gaulle's political style
        A.   caused him to assume official leadership of the Gaullist party
        B.   favored the strong role of parliament
       *C.   disdained the role of interest groups and narrow partisanship
        D.   deemphasized French sovereignty
        E.   reflected the moderation of French communism

Completion Questions

1. The conservative writer Joseph de Maistre disparaged the <u>WRITTEN</u> elements
    of a living constitution.

2. The eighteenth-century French thinker who established the doctrine of the
    separation of powers was <u>MONTESQUIEU</u>.

3. Among the crises that often lead to constitutional dictatorship are
    foreign war, internal rebellion, natural disasters, and <u>DEPRESSION</u>.

4. Most cases reach the United States Supreme Court through its <u>APPELLATE</u>
    jurisdiction.

5. The branch of law that has special relevance for bureaucratic activities
    is known as <u>ADMINSTRATIVE</u> law.

6. What Americans call the Administration is known as the <u>GOVERNMENT</u> in
    parliamentary regimes.

7. Cabinet members without specific departmental responsibilities are called
    ministers without <u>PORTFOLIO</u>.

8. The collegial nature of cabinets involves the notion of collective
    cabinet <u>RESPONSIBILITY</u>.

9. The West German proviso that the lower house must name a new chancellor when it votes out the old one is known as the CONSTRUCTIVE vote of nonconfidence.

10. The Scandinavian countries are unique because they feature UNICAMERAL legislatures.

11. The French Economic and Social Council is a weak version of a SOCIOECONOMIC chamber.

12. Weak upper houses often have what is called a SUSPENSIVE veto over legislation.

13. In West Germany the special bureau that helps the Bundestag's presiding officer is the Council of ELDERS.

14. A, B, C, D, and E refer to STANDING committees in the British House of Commons.

15. In French constitutional thinking laws are general in scope, while DECREES cover more specific matters.

16. European interpellations, British questions, and American investigations refer to the parliamentary function of OVERSIGHT of administration.

17. The American president does not possess an ITEM veto.

18. The ADMINISTRATIVE constituency of the American president consists of the vast and sprawling federal bureaucracy.

19. According to James D. Barber, presidential performance is largely the outcome of personality variables like character, style, and WORLDVIEW.

20. In Barber's typology, a president characterized by self-concern, perfectionism, and denial of self-gratification among other things is doubtless an ACTIVE-NEGATIVE president.

21. Early setbacks to Roosevelt's New Deal were delivered by the SUPREME COURT.

22. While the United States Constitution refers to officials who report to the president, it does not specifically mention a CABINET.

23. In addition to the State Department, the American president receives foreign policy advice from the NATIONAL SECURITY Council.

24. One advantage the French president has over his American counterpart is his role in initiating REFERENDUMS on either constitutional amendments or broad policy issues.

25. General de Gaulle was head of the PROVISIONAL government in France in 1944-46.

26. A crisis that almost toppled President de Gaulle in the early 1960s involved self-determination for <u>ALGERIA</u>.

27. The Swiss Federal Council is our best current example of the <u>PLURAL</u> executive.

28. The party composition of the Swiss Federal Council is presently called the <u>MAGIC</u> formula.

29. In the 1970s those who were alarmed at the power of the American president often spoke of the <u>IMPERIAL</u> presidency.

30. Differences of political <u>CULTURE</u> may help explain why constitutionalism has an easier time in western-oriented societies.

True-False Questions

1. If a British politician violates a convention of the British Constitution, he can be removed by judicial impeachment. (F)

2. Montesquieu's theory of the separation of powers was based on the three estates of the French monarchy. (F)

3. Constitutional dictatorship, which is by intention a temporary expedient, can leave lasting traces on the constitutional fabric of a country. (T)

4. In West German judicial review, the Federal Supreme Court is the constitutional counterpart of the United States Supreme Court. (F)

5. In the parliamentary system the head of government is a merely ceremonial leader. (F)

6. Contemporary Italy shows how far modern parliamentarism has departed from the classic model. (F)

7. In the parliamentary system any defeat absolutely requires that the government either resign or call for new elections. (F)

8. It is the growth of government per se that largely accounts for the changes involved in the "executive revolution" or the decline of parliaments. (T)

9. The resignations of British prime ministers like Neville Chamberlain in 1940, Anthony Eden in 1957, and Harold Macmillan in 1963 all resulted from nonconfidence votes in the House of Commons. (F)

10. Joint committees are essential to the workings of unicameral legislatures. (F)

11. Whips are the top assistants to the presiding officer in parliaments. (F)

12. The United States involvement in the Korean War of 1950–53 followed President Truman's declaration of war. (F)

13. One reason why French presidents are perhaps more deserving of the label "chief legislator" than American presidents is the results of French parliamentary elections. (T)

14. Charles de Gaulle resigned in 1946 and 1969 because respect for the French Constitution legally required it. (F)

15. The Swiss president is elected by popular vote for a four-year term. (F)

The overall theme of this chapter concerns the spread of bureaucracy and what this means for the modern state. First we discuss the Weberian model of bureaucracy and the pathologies that allegedly refute Weber's claims about the efficiency and effectiveness of bureaucratic organization. Covering administration was always one of the driest topics in political science so that focusing in on the pathologies could liven things up substantially. The works by Parkinson and Peter are in this vein, while Anthony Downs's typology of officials who systematically distort information to their superiors is interesting. (See Suggestions.) An attempt to defend bureaucratic performance in America is the theme of Charles T. Goodsell's The Case for Bureaucracy (Chatham, N.J.: Chatham House, 1983).

Also important is the whole question of corruption and the specific relevance of this problem for Third World countries. Here the Heidenheimer collection in the Suggestions is priceless. The general problem of Third World bureaucracies is covered in both case-study and theoretical approaches in the anthologies by Bendix and Schmidt et al. in the Suggestions.

Regarding committee decision making doubtless the Groupthink motif is the most interesting. Janis's book is essential and he even brought out a brief film on GT some years ago.

Two overarching themes that receive modest attention in the text could be explored in greater detail: (1) the old dichotomy between politics and administration; and (2) the humanistic critique of bureaucracy that looks to self-management (see Vanek in Suggestions). On this Michels's "iron law of oligarchy" would make a good counterpoint.

1. For Max Weber the essence of bureaucracy is
   A. pathology
   B. charisma
   *C. rationality
   D. notables
   E. patrimonialism

2. Chairman Mao's attempt to dislodge Chinese bureaucracy in the 1960s is known as
   A. the Long March
   B. thought reform
   C. the Great Leap Forward
   D. the Sino-Soviet dispute
   *E. the Cultural Revolution

3. Which of the following is not a component of the Weberian model of bureaucracy?
   A. written documentation
   B. systematic division of labor
   *C. collegial administration
   D. state funding
   E. administrative hierarchy

4. Which best symbolizes the stress on bureaucratic routine practices?
   *A. SOP
   B. ZBB
   C. DOT
   D. PPBS
   E. MBO

5. The notion of chain-of-command best reflects
   A. systematic division of labor
   *B. definite administrative hierarchy
   C. state funding
   D. technical training
   E. no ownership of office

6. Appointing people to office through family or friendship considerations is
   A. peculation
   B. the Peter principle
   C. nonfeasance
   D. bribery
   *E. nepotism

7. Parkinson's law is concerned with
   A. red tape
   B. delegation of authority
   C. corruption
   *D. inefficiency
   E. the Peter principle

8. The Peter principle would afflict bureaucracy most particularly regarding
   A. SOP
   B. division of labor
   *C. administrative hierarchy
   D. continuity of business
   E. state funding

9. According to Anthony Downs bureaucratic officials distort the upward flow of information because
   A. of normal human error
   B. of Parkinson's Law
   *C. of a variety of selfish and other motives

D. they do not have reliable information
E. of thematic apperception

10. In Down's typology, officials who distort because of their dedication to the public interest are
   A. advocates   D. zealots
   *B. statesmen   E. climbers
   C. conservers

11. The expression "bureaucro-syndicalism" most clearly suggests that
   A. bureaucracy rules the modern state
   B. Kafka was right about bureaucracy
   *C. public sector unionization may alter the policy process
   D. the Weberian model is irrelevant
   E. Third World administration has special features

12. An "executive minister"
   *A. relishes internal matters like structure, personnel, and morale
   B. has cabinet rank
   C. is the chief assistant to the political department head
   D. monopolizes departmental policymaking
   E. would rather be working somewhere else

13. The chief concern of the "ambassador minister" is probably with
   A. foreign countries   D. policy selection
   B. the ministry of external affairs   E. policy initiation
   *C. clientele groups

14. Which service cannot be provided for the politically-appointed minister by his permanent bureaucratic staff?
   A. policy implementation   *D. political campaigning
   B. political advice   E. liaison with clienteles
   C. mutual political protection

15. The "politics of consulation" suggests most closely
   A. legislative-executive relations
   B. advisory judicial opinions
   C. bureaucro-syndicalism
   D. referendums and initiatives
   *E. officials seeking interest-group input

16. Cooptation means
   A. bogus consultation
   B. promotion through nepotism
   C. interagency exchange of information
   *D. bringing outside elements into the leadership
   E. public sector unionization

17. Which of the following cannot be considered part of the informal leadership of committees?
   *A. the secretary   D. the task leader
   B. the social leader   E. all of the above
   C. the gadfly

18. Groupthink is most likely to afflict
    A. parliament   D. a representative committee
    *B. a highly cohesive committee   E. a legislative committee
    C. a consultative committee

19. Which is not a chief symptom of Groupthink?
    A. an illusion of invulnerability
    B. self-censorship
    C. an illusion of unanimity
    D. a mindguard
    *E. a gadfly

20. One way to head off Groupthink before it really develops is
    *A. for the leader to withhold his personal preference
    B. to disband the committee when it first surfaces
    C. to fire all yes-men and "nodders"
    D. to replace the human element with computers
    E. to change the advice from binding to nonbinding

21. According to Max Weber patrimonialism is a kind of halfway house between
    bureaucracy and
    A. charisma   D. syndicalism
    *B. feudalism   E. post-industrial society
    C. administration by notables

22. Patron-client relations are
    A. on an equal basis   D. peculiar to medieval feudalism
    *B. highly personalistic   E. essentially capitalistic
    C. alien to patrimonialism

23. The "revolutionary" changes of the last fifteen years in Peru have not
    *A. eliminated clientelistic relationships
    B. encouraged shanty towns
    C. launched mobilization efforts
    D. brought in the military
    E. instituted SINAMOS

24. An official who handles citizen complaints about bureaucratic misdeeds
    often is called
    A. a patron   D. a magistrate
    *B. an ombudsman   E. an apostate
    C. a Sinamos

25. The classic dichotomy between politics and administration is originally
    attributed to
    A. Max Weber   D. C. Northcote Parkinson
    B. Irving Janis   E. none of the above
    *C. Woodrow Wilson

Completion Questions

1. Max Weber felt that the true ruler in the modern state was the
    <u>BUREAUCRACY</u>.

2. In the Weberian model of bureaucracy, there would be a systematic
    division of <u>LABOR</u>.

3. Bureaucracies generally measure "merit" for hiring or promotion by
    <u>EXAMINATIONS</u>.

4. The <u>PATHOLOGIES</u> of bureaucracy explain why their performance is often
    below what the Weberian model suggests.

5. The old-time political <u>MACHINES</u> may have been corrupt but they helped to
    humanize and personalize assistance to the needy.

6. The expression "<u>SPAN</u> of control" refers to the number of people under the
    direct control and supervision of an official.

7. <u>PETER</u> taught that "in a hierarchy every employee tends to rise to his
    level of incompetence."

8. The tendency of officials to alter the information they transmit upwards
    in a hierarchy is called <u>DISTORTION</u>.

9. The <u>CLIMBER</u> is an official who distorts in order to raise his chances for
    promotion.

10. The <u>ZEALOT</u> is an official who distorts because he is obsessed by some
    cause.

11. When the tormenters of Kafka's Joseph K. assure him that they have
    nothing personally against him, this illustrates the <u>IMPERSONAL</u> nature of
    bureaucracy.

12. When a government minister enters office with a ready-made set of
    policy-proposals, he is a <u>POLICY INITIATOR</u>.

13. When the minister asks his staff for suggestions and then chooses among
    them, he is a <u>POLICY-SELECTOR</u>.

14. A minister with a "management textbook view" of his job is an <u>EXECUTIVE</u>
    minister.

15. An <u>AMBASSADOR</u> minister is nearly obsessed with the "external relations"
    of his ministry.

16. While neither their hearts nor their heads are in the job, <u>MINIMALISTS</u>
    accept titular responsibility for their ministry.

17. A ministerial staff can help with the consultations and negotiations
    involved with consensus making and <u>CONFLICT-MANAGEMENT</u>.

18. Bringing in interest-group representatives in early stages of policy formulation is called CONSULTATION.

19. The GADFLY can be considered the self-appointed conscience of a committee.

20. In the Groupthink situation, a MINDGUARD often keeps out ideas and opinions that disrupt the apparent consensus.

21. Designating a so-called DEVIL'S ADVOCATE to give expression to unpopular opinions can cut down on Groupthink.

22. Students of Third World countries suggest that PERSONAL rulership or governance occurs when the preconditions for modern bureaucratic organization are lacking.

23. A single patron can have a large number of CLIENTS.

24. In most Third World countries the political significance of tribal, kinship, and sectarian bonds remains stronger than in the typical WESTERN or communist country.

25. Many people who advocate formal organizational democracy are inspired by the system of SELF-MANAGEMENT in Yugoslavia.

True-False Questions

1. In the Weberian schema, charisma was inherently conservative, while bureaucracy was a dynamic and even revolutionary force. (F)

2. In the Weberian model of bureaucracy, rules and regulations impede the overall rationality of the organization. (F)

3. The term "red tape" originated in the context of bureaucracy's need to document its activities. (T)

4. Corruption is another name for the abuse of power. (F)

5. That the leaders of most organizations were unprepared for their jobs illustrates Parkinson's Law. (F)

6. Normal human error in conjunction with hierarchical distortion largely explains why officials often receive poor quality information. (T)

7. The advocate is an official who distorts information to his bosses in the interest of some moral, political, or religious principle. (F)

8. Kafka's The Trial illustrates what happens when the so-called merit principle is applied without broader considerations in a bureaucratic organization. (F)

9. Bureaucro-syndicalism is simply a result of the growth of the modern welfare state. (F)

10. In Japan we find that many ministers have previous service in the bureaucracy. (T)

11. Political appointees **and** permanent civil servants could easily exchange roles. (F)

12. Resort to committee-style decision making is intended to narrow the scope of information in policy formulation. (F)

13. Frequent use of cooptation suggests that the consultative process is being used for purposes other than information gathering. (T)

14. Groupthink occurs because rivalries and intrigues among the members of a committee cause decisions to follow a "hidden agenda." (F)

15. In classic patrimonialism the ruler has succeeded in depriving the old nobility of some of its rights and autonomy. (T)

This chapter starts out with the contrast between dictatorship and constitutionalism and moves then to that between totalitarian and authoritarian dictatorship. On this latter issue there is a wealth of material in Juan Linz, "Totalitarian and Authoritarian Regimes," in <u>Handbook of Political Science</u>, vol. 3 (Addison-Wesley).

On military regimes the literature is divided between the analysis of coups and the regimes themselves. Edward Luttwak, <u>Coup D'Etat</u> (Greenwich, Conn.: Fawcett, 1969) is a good theoretical analysis written from the standpoint of a "how to" manual. This edition of the text plays down the "military and modernization" issue, though lectures might want to go into this--a caveat is the can of worms that "modernization" as a concept involves. Some good case studies were produced by Alfred Stepan on Brazil (note 29 in text) and on Peru, <u>The State and Society: Peru in Comparative Perspective</u> (Princeton: Princeton University Press, 1978). A recent collection by Amos Perlmutter and Valerie P. Bennett, <u>The Political Influence of the Military: A Comparative Perspective</u> (New Haven: Yale University Press, 1980) has an abundance of theoretical and empirical materials.

On the single-party see the anthologies by Dahl and by Huntington and Moore in the Suggestions. See also the books cited in notes 31 and 33.

1. While totalitarian regimes thrive on ideology, authoritarian regimes rely more on a
   *A. mentality
   B. power structure
   C. worldview
   D. myth
   E. religion

2. Authoritarian systems often show an autonomous
   A. party
   B. foreign policy
   *C. military
   D. elite
   E. leader

3. The traditional American view that the military must be kept under the thumb of the civil authorities is called
   *A. the liberal model
   B. the professional model
   C. the praetorian model
   D. the non-interventionist model
   E. the separatist model

4. The three types (or stages) of praetorianism are oligarchical, middle-class, and
   A. democratic
   *B. mass
   C. Roman
   D. liberal
   E. communist

5. The military ouster of Juan Peron in Argentina in 1955 is a classic case of a
   A. reform coup
   B. breakthrough coup
   C. praetorian coup
   D. counterrevolutionary coup
   *E. veto coup

6. When the military sees the civilian leadership as weak, corrupt, and self-indulgent, it shows their own
   A. hypernationalism
   B. integral nationalism
   C. chauvinism
   *D. puritanism
   E. patriotism

7. The antipolitics aspect of the military mentality refers most nearly to
   A. economic planning
   *B. disdain for political wheeling-and-dealing
   C. hatred for ideologies
   D. collective decision making
   E. chain-of-command

8. Idi Amin was not
   A. a soldier
   B. originally trained in Israel
   *C. a Christian
   D. a member of a small tribe
   E. popular in any respect

9. One rather popular policy of Idi Amin was expulsion of the
   A. British
   *B. Asians
   C. Communists
   D. Soviets
   E. Libyans

10. The traditional role of the Brazilian military involving intervention and then return to the barracks illustrates the
    A. liberal model
    *B. moderator model
    C. professional model
    D. ruler model
    E. praetorian model

11. In 1964 the Brazilian military ousted the leftist president
    A. Vargas
    B. Peron
    *C. Goulart
    D. Castello Branco
    E. Costa e Silva

12. The two contrasting patterns of the single-party's relationship to the society at large are the
    *A. mobilizational and pluralistic
    B. ruler and moderator
    C. authoritarian and totalitarian
    D. oligarchic and democratic
    E. exoteric and esoteric

13. To determine the dominance or subordination of a single-party vis-a-vis the government we look to
    A. ideology, leadership, polity
    B. legitimation, participation, policy
    *C. legitimation, leadership, policy
    D. participation, ideology, organization
    E. participation, legitimation, ideology

14. From the standpoint of the single-party, personalities, churches, bureaucracies, parliaments, and economic groupings make up so many
    A. extensions
    *B. power rivals
    C. auxiliary organizations
    D. governments
    E. subcommittees

15. Which of the following competed with the single-party (PNF) in providing legitimacy for Mussolini's Italy?
    *A. the monarchy
    B. the Italian Communist party
    C. the president
    D. the corporate state
    E. Adolph Hitler

16. Mussolini's first public office in Italy was
    A. Duce of Fascism
    *B. prime minister
    C. president
    D. Mayor of Milan
    E. head of the chamber of deputies

17. What political party did the young Mussolini belong to?
    A. anarchist
    B. nationalist
    *C. socialist
    D. national socialist
    E. communist

18. What was Mussolini's profession when he became a national figure?
    A. professional soldier
    B. college professor
    C. novelist
    *D. newspaper editor
    E. paper-hanger

19. In 1924 what crisis moved Mussolini's government closer to an outright dictatorship?
    A. the Lateran pact
    *B. the Matteoti affair
    C. the great depression
    D. the Libyan war
    E. the Munich Crisis

20. The second half of Mussolini's dictatorship was marked by his increasing subordination to
    A. King Victor Emmanuel
    B. his brother Arnaldo
    C. the Pope
    *D. Adolph Hitler
    E. his mistress

21. Which institution survived all of Mussolini's transformations and even voiced dissent on occasion?
    A. the Chamber of Deputies
    *B. the Senate
    C. the Cabinet
    D. the referendum
    E. the Privy Council

22. As is generally the case with dictatorships, Mussolini's cabinet could be described as
    A. a coalition government
    *B. a group of the leader's administrative assistants
    C. a collegial policymaker
    D. responsible to parliament
    E. abolished after a few shaky years

23. The Council of Fasci and Corporations is best described as
    A. Mussolini's cabinet
    B. the central committee of the PNF
    *C. the Fascist legislature
    D. the Grand Council of Fascism
    E. a popular-approved list of 400 delegates

24. Which group did temporarily display some policy impact under Mussolini?
    A. the Chamber of Deputies
    B. the Senate
    *C. the Grand Council of Fascism
    D. the National Council
    E. the Committee of Public Safety

25. The principle underlying the corporative state was
    A. to overthrow the capitalist system
    B. to reunify church and state
    C. to ensure public ownership of the means of production
    D. to make corporations public
    *E. to overcome the conflict between labor and capital

Completion Questions

1. The contrast between dictatorship and constitutionalism revolves not

around limits to power in general, but specifically around <u>LEGAL</u> limits to power.

2. The underlying social policy of totalitarian dictatorship can be called total <u>REVOLUTION</u>.

3. A crucial difference between authoritarian and totalitarian dictatorship involves inner versus outer <u>CONFORMITY</u>.

4. Totalitarianism requires the <u>SUBORDINATION</u> of the military.

5. In a praetorian society political and administrative bodies suffer from a low level of <u>INSTITUTIONALIZATION</u>.

6. When the military justifies its coup by attacking the previous civilian regime's betrayal of the national interest, its mentality exhibits <u>HYPERNATIONALISM</u>.

7. The <u>COLLECTIVISM</u> of the military mentality can result in a preference for "socialism" or a "command economy."

8. The Brazilian president who was twice removed from power by military coups was <u>VARGAS</u>.

9. The military regime in Brazil could claim some success in the area of <u>ECONOMIC</u> development.

10. When the government actually controls the single-party, the latter is <u>SUBORDINATE</u>.

11. In addition to legitimation and recruitment functions, a dominant single-party would supervise all stages of the <u>POLICY</u> process.

12. Perhaps the most serious power rival to the Fascist Party in Italy was <u>MUSSOLINI</u>.

13. The great social theorist whose lectures in Switzerland were attended by Mussolini was <u>PARETO</u>.

14. In October of 1922 occurred the fabled <u>MARCH</u> on Rome.

15. After 1936 the world could speak of the Rome-Berlin <u>AXIS</u>.

16. After the German occupation of Italy, Hitler installed Mussolini as head of the so-called Italian <u>SOCIAL</u> Republic.

17. Mussolini's behavior often seemed to reflect his youthful reading of the German philosopher <u>NIETZSCHE</u>.

18. In 1923 the Acerbo reform in Italy provided that the party with at least <u>TWENTY-FIVE</u> percent of the votes would get two-thirds of the seats in the Chamber of Deputies.

19. Using phony elections and stooge parliaments for outpourings of pomp,

pageantry, and political ritualism relates to the <u>SYMBOLIC</u> functions performed by legislative bodies in dictatorships.

20. The <u>QUADRUMVIRS</u> were four old-line Fascists who were made life-members of the <u>Grand</u> Council of Fascism.

21. The Party Directorate was the <u>SECRETARIAT</u> of the PNF and included the party secretary and eight others.

22. The councilors of the twenty-two national corporations together made up the General <u>ASSEMBLY</u> of the National Council of Corporations.

23. Like so many other institutions in Fascist Italy, the elaborate corporative apparatus played a more decorative or <u>CHOREOGRAPHIC</u> role than a true policy role.

24. Ancient near-eastern and far-eastern authoritarian monarchies are called oriental <u>DESPOTISMS</u>.

25. Those who see modernization in social and political terms tend to think the <u>SINGLE-PARTY</u> performed fairly well.

True-False Questions

1. All forms of dictatorship resemble each other in all significant respects more than any of them resemble constitutional regimes. (F)

2. The social policy of authoritarian dictatorships can run the gamut from reactionary to revolutionary and all stops in between. (T)

3. The post-Stalin shift from military subordination to accommodation is one aspect of the persistent strength of Soviet totalitarianism. (F)

4. In oligarchical praetorianism the politically-relevant public is highly restrictive. (T)

5. Idi Amin is a good modern-day example of the ancient Roman dictator. (F)

6. In 1964 the Brazilian military appeared to shift from following the ruler model to assuming the moderator model of military politics. (F)

7. A pluralistic single-party tends to deemphasize any ideological mission. (T)

8. In addition to Mussolini's personalism, the PNF's aspirations for a dominant role were obstructed by the ideological principle of statism. (T)

9. Mussolini led an exemplary middle-class personal life. (F)

10. 1939 marked the high-point of Mussolini's dictatorship. (F)

11. Mussolini's ouster in July 1943 was accomplished by an uprising led by communist partisans. (F)

12. The Fascist militia posed no threat to the regular Italian army. (T)

13. After the March on Rome of October 1922 the Fascists quickly dismantled all the pre-Fascist institutions and proclaimed a new Fascist constitution. (F)

14. Fascism really did not discredit corporative experiments; it never really tried them. (T)

15. It is clear that the military is a far more effective agent of modernization than is the single-party. (F)

This chapter has (1) a fairly extensive discussion of the notion of totalitarianism followed by (2) a discussion of two "case studies":   Nazi Germany and Stalinist Russia.   The classic works on totalitarianism are, of course, Arendt's The Origins of Totalitarianism, Friedrich and Brzezinski's Totalitarian Dictatorship and Autocracy (especially the 1956 edition), and Sigmund Neumann, Permanent Revolution--all cited in the Suggestions.   The essays by Barber and Curtis in Totalitarianism in Perspective: Three Views represent recent criticism of the notion of totalitarianism.   The Friedrich-Brzezinski syndrome is still a good way to broach the topic with students, even if critical conclusions are reached about it.   Again Juan Linz's contribution to vol. 3 of the Handbook of Political Science is excellent for both an exhaustive survey of the literature and a mammoth bibliography.

On Stalin's USSR, two works seem outstanding: the 1953 edition of Merle Fainsod's How Russia is Ruled, and Leonard Schapiro's The Communist Party of the Soviet Union (see Suggestions).   Also, Robert Tucker has edited a book titled Stalinism.

On Nazi Germany, Franz Neumann's Behemoth; Bracher's The German Dictatorship; and Peterson's The Limits of Hitler's Power treat the Nazi phenomenon from rather different perspectives.

If the instructor wishes to pursue the psychohistorical approach to Stalin and Huntington, he or she should see the works cited in text notes 49 to 58.

1. Which of the following is not part of the original Friedrich-Brzezinski totalitarian syndrome?
    A. totalist/utopian ideology
    B. command economy
    *C. regime-directed youth movement
    D. weapons monopoly
    E. monopoly of mass communications

2. The official Soviet doctrine of art criticism is called
    A. Soviet Idealism   D. futurism
    B. proletarian consciousness   E. art for art's sake
    *C. Socialist Realism

3. Instead of "ideology" the Nazis preferred to call their doctrine
    A. Bewusstsein   D. Philosophie
    B. Uberbau   *E. Weltanschauung
    C. Dialektic

4. Perhaps the branch of natural science most liable to infiltration from a totalitarian ideology is
    A. mathematics   D. physics
    *B. biology   E. ecology
    C. chemistry

5. Which of the following does not figure in Sigmund Neumann's 1942 list of the functions of the dictatorial party?
    A. creating the political elite
    B. controlling and educating the masses
    *C. supervising economic production
    D. maintaining communications between state and society
    E. none of the above

6. GPU, NKVD, MVD are all organizations of the
    A. military   D. totalitarian movement
    *B. secret police   E. Nazi party
    C. communist party

7. The Chinese Communists have generally avoided extremes of terrorism by using sophisticated techniques like
    A. neutralization   D. reinforcement
    *B. thought reform   E. articulation
    C. class consciousness

8. The best description of a paramilitary organization is a
    A. secret police   D. veterans group
    B. the Red army   E. pacifist committee
    *C. private army

9. Which of the following is not argued against the traditional notion of totalitarianism?
    A. it is an ideological cold war weapon

B. it is obsolete
C. it underestimates the regime's susceptibility to pressures
*D. it equates modern totalitarianism with oriental despotism
E. it oversimplifies the power structure

10. The supposedly monopolistic or monolithic character of totalitarianism encounters serious limits in the notion of islands of
*A. separateness
B. autonomy
C. independence
D. nonconformity
E. imperviousness

11. Stalin relaxed some of the restrictions on the Russian Orthodox Church in exchange for its full support in
A. the collectivization drive
*B. World War II
C. the Afghanistan occupation
D. the Sino-Soviet dispute
E. the Korean conflict

12. The first leader of the Soviet regime was
A. Stalin
*B. Lenin
C. Trotsky
D. Marx
E. Engels

13. The period 1918-1921 in soviet history is known as
A. the Great Patriotic War
B. the collectivization drive
C. the Great Purge
*D. War Communism
E. the Reign of Terror

14. In Soviet history NEP stands for
A. National Ethnic Party
B. the secret police
*C. New Economic Policy
D. the party praesidium
E. Council of People's Commissars

15. The four pillars of Stalinist totalitarian rule were
A. the party, the church, the army, the intelligentsia
*B. the party, the government, the army, the secret police
C. the party, the intelligentsia, the secret police, the army
D. the party, the church, big business, the landowners
E. the party, the intelligentsia, the secret police, the church

16. The "legislative organ" of the CPSU is the
A. Supreme Soviet
B. Council of Ministers
C. Central Committee
D. Praesidium
*E. Party Congress

17. Which of the following was never part of the formal organization of the CPSU?
A. Politburo
B. Orgburo
C. Secretariat
D. Central Committee
*E. KGB

18. In the 1930s Yagoda and Yezhov were two Soviet
A. biologists
B. premiers
C. heads of state
D. party secretaries
*E. secret police chiefs

19. Which of the following affords one delegate for every 300,000 people?
    A. the Party Congress   *D. the Soviet of the Union
    B. the Soviet of Nationalities   E. the Praesidium
    C. Central Committee

20. The current technical name of the Soviet "cabinet" is
    A. Praesidium of the Supreme Soviet
    *B. Praesidium of the Council of Ministers
    C. Praesidium of the Central Committee
    D. Council of Peoples Commissars
    E. the Secretariat of the CPSU

21. Political commissars
    *A. check on the military
    B. serve in the SS
    C. serve in the Party Congress
    D. are candidate members of the central committee
    E. are KGB agents

22. In the USSR "collective leadership" is supposed to counter
    A. the cult of personality   D. polycentrism
    *B. the private enterprise system   E. socialist legality
    C. state farms

23. Leonid Breshnev twice served as
    A. premier
    B. Secretary-General of the CPSU
    C. head of the KGB
    *D. Chairman of Supreme Soviet Praesidium
    E. head of Soviet UN delegation

24. Von Bruning, von Papen, and von Schleicher were
    A. prominent Nazis
    B. in Hitler's first cabinet
    C. German presidents before Hitler
    *D. German Chancellors before Hitler
    E. slain in the purge of June 1934

25. In the early years the number-two man in Nazi Germany was
    A. Martin Bormann   D. Heinrich Himmler
    B. Josef Goebbels   E. Ernst Roehm
    *C. Hermann Goering

26. The SA was
    *A. the stormtroopers   D. the German Army
    B. the Nazi party   E. the German Air Force
    C. the secret police

27. The leaders of the geographical units of the Nazi party were called
    A. Fuhrerprinzip   D. commissars
    *B. Gauleiter   E. Lander
    C. Reichstatthalter

28. By ethnic origin Joseph Stalin was a(n)
    A. Jew   D. Great Russian
    B. Armenian   E. Austrian
  *C. Georgian

29. A favorite tactic of Stalin in his rese to power in the mid-1920s was to
    A. point out Lenin's mistakes
  *B. portray himself as a middle-of-the-roader
    C. seek the office of Soviet president
    D. favor an alliance with Germany
    E. resign his post as Secretary-General of the CPSU

30. A pretext Hitler used to crush political opposition was
    A. the assassination of President von Hindenburg
    B. the Ribbentrop-Molotov Pact
    C. the collapse of the German mark
  *D. the burning of the Reichstag building
    E. the foundation of the State of Israel

Completion Questions

1. Pasternak's Nobel Prize-winning novel DR. ZHIVAGO was officially attacked
    in the USSR because it failed to meet regime standards.

2. Many view totalitarian ideologies as secular RELIGIONS.

3. Hannah Arendt considered the symbiotic relationship between ideology and
    TERROR as the essence of totalitarian rule.

4. Under totalitarian rule, when government or party agents screen material
    before it reaches the public, it is called PRECENSORSHIP.

5. Because it characterizes the modern STATE, a weapons monopoly seems a
    rather weak component of a totalitarian syndrome.

6. As a sort of island of separateness ETHNIC groups can form a stumbling
    block for a totalitarian elite.

7. The Soviet Communist party was originally known as the BOLSHEVIK party.

8. Stalin's main rival in the struggle for power after Lenin's death was
    TROTSKY.

9. The Supreme Soviet chooses a small board called its PRAESIDIUM to carry
    on between sessions of the parent body.

10. UNION-Republic ministries have separate organizations at both the
    national (Moscow) and republican levels.

11. KHRUSHCHEV made the famous "anti-Stalin" speech at the Twentieth Party
    Congress in 1956.

12. The Soviet secret police is now called the KGB, which means <u>COMMITTEE</u> of State Security.

13. Sovnarkhozy refers to Khrushchev's regional <u>ECONOMIC</u> councils.

14. Hitler wished to be known as <u>FUHRER</u> and Chancellor of the German people.

15. The Nazi parliament was known as the <u>REICHSTAG</u>.

16. The organizational core of the NSDAP was the PO, or <u>POLITICAL</u> Organization.

17. The secret state police in Nazi Germany was known as the <u>GESTAPO</u>.

18. <u>HIMMLER</u> was always head of the SS.

19. Dr. Robert Ley was head of the German <u>LABOR</u> Front.

20. Adolph Hitler was born in <u>AUSTRIA</u>.

21. Lenin was first attracted to Stalin because of his supposed expertise on the <u>NATIONAL</u> question.

22. Stalin used the slogan "<u>SOCIALISM</u> in one country" in his struggle against Trotsky.

23. Stalin met something of his match in President <u>TITO</u> of Yugoslavia, who broke with the Soviets in 1948.

24. Hitler's early ambition was to be a(n) <u>ARTIST</u>.

25. The full name of the Nazi party was the National Socialist German <u>WORKERS</u> party.

26. Hitler's abortive attempt to seize power in 1923 is known as the <u>MUNICH</u> Beer Hall putsch.

27. In 1932, Hitler lost the presidential election to the aged Paul von <u>HINDENBURG</u>.

28. The <u>MUNICH</u> conference of 1938 produced the dismemberment of Czechoslovakia.

29. Robert Tucker refers to the <u>WARFARE</u> personality, which can rise to leadership in organizations during severe periods of stress.

30. A paranoid personality general sees evil <u>CONSPIRACIES</u> against him and his group.

True-False Questions

1. Modern totalitarianism is no more and no less than a perennial threat to human liberty that has surfaced from the beginnings of human civilization. (F)

2. Friedrich and Brzezinski suggested that Fascist and Communist totalitarian dictatorships are "basically alike." (T)

3. Totalitarian ideology is brutally realistic; there is nothing visionary about it. (F)

4. The totalitarian party is the institution which has either liquidated or coordinated all possible competitors. (F)

5. Terror always reflects the phobias of basically sick personalities. (F)

6. Censorship of the printed word is neither new nor peculiar to totalitarian dictatorships. (T)

7. Most industry in Nazi Germany was privately owned. (T)

8. Stalin was so frightened of a military coup that he viciously purged the military in 1928. (F)

9. The first Soviet Five-Year Plan marked the end of the NEP. (T)

10. As long as he lived, Stalin never relinquished his post as Secretary-General of the CPSU. (T)

11. Nikita Khrushchev, Stalin's first successor, assumed the office of premier upon the old dictator's death in March 1953. (F)

12. Ironically, Hitler was the sole Nazi in his first cabinet in early 1933. (F)

13. Hitler was totally incapable of delegating administrative tasks to his subordinates. (F)

14. The SA actually sent front-line units to fight during World War II. (F)

15. Hitler worked as a political intelligence officer for the Austro-Hungarian army. (F)

Chapter 6: Social Movements and Revolution

This chapter has two main concerns: (1) it looks at some theories and types of social movements; and (2) it focuses on the problem of revolution. Though it seems clear that such phenomena are of great importance to comparative political science, most texts tend to minimize or omit treatment of them.

For theoretical material on collective behavior and especially social movements, see various contributions to G. Lindzey and E. Aronson, eds., Handbook of Social Psychology, vol. 4 (Reading, Mass.: Addison-Wesley, 1969); and to R.E.L. Faris, ed., Handbook of Modern Sociology (Chicago: Rand-McNally, 1964). In the Suggestions the books by Kornhauser, Hoffer, and Lanternari are somewhat less jargonistic than the previous sources. The case studies on social movements are, of course, legion, but Cohn's The Pursuit of the Millenium is crucial.

The literature on revolution is equally vast, but the works by Brinton, Hagopian, and Skocpol in the Suggestions cover most of the prevailing points of view.

This chapter provides an opportunity for the instructor to bring some special areas of expertise or interest into the course. Revolutions is one topic, but the psychological aspects of politics or the debate between the orthodox and the revisionist view of social movements seem fair game too. Also perusal of notes will provide some special sources.

Multiple-Choice Questions

1. The classic theory of "crowd psychology" was developed by the French
   sociologist
   A. Emile Durkheim   D. Marcel Marceau
   *B. Gustave Le Bon   E. Alexis de Tocqueville
   C. Claude Levi-Strauss

2. Which theory of crowds maintains that people lose their personal
   identities as crowd members?
   A. convergence theory   D. unconventional theory
   *B. contagion theory   E. spontaneous theory
   C. collective theory

3. The third phase in the life-cycle approach to social movements is
   A. incubation   D. structuralization
   *B. adaptation   E. equilibrium
   C. action

4. Eric Hoffer's "men of words" have also been called
   A. practical men of action   D. incubators
   B. fanatics   *E. ideologists
   C. administrators

5. Georges Sorel is most associated with the term
   A. fanatic   *D. myth
   B. social movement   E. prophet
   C. crowd psychology

6. What do we call those members of a movement who possess "inner knowledge"
   of the leader's message?
   *A. disciples   D. neophytes
   B. fanatics   E. sympathizers
   C. militant following

7. Which type of factor is heavily stressed by the "orthodox" approach to
   social movements
   A. sociological   D. political
   B. ideological   E. economic
   *C. psychological

8. Millenary movements are generally inspired by
   A. Marxism   D. racism
   B. national humiliations   E. oxymoronism
   *C. Biblical prophecies

9. The Reverend Jim Jones headed a
   *A. messianic movement   D. protest movement
   B. youth movement   E. Congressional delegation
   C. nativistic movement

10. In the spring of 1968 the Gaullist government in France was confronted by
    a

39

A.	coup d'etat	*D.	youth movement
B.	nativistic revolt	E.	communist insurrection
C.	messiah		

11. Revivalist nativism features
    - A. reformism
    - B. modern nationalism
    - C. Marxism-Leninism
    - D. totalitarianism
    - *E. total rejection of the alien

12. A violent, illegal attempt to seize or expand political power is a
    - A. revolt
    - B. revolution
    - *C. coup d'etat
    - D. social movement
    - E. sedition

13. It is a mistake to conceive of revolt as a
    - *A. failed revolution
    - B. social movement
    - C. violent upheaval
    - D. restorative movement
    - E. form of subrevolutionary violence

14. The Khomeini movement in Iran cannot be characterized as
    - A. a revolt
    - B. millenary
    - C. nativistic
    - D. republican
    - *E. Sunni

15. The late Shah of Iran's secret police was known as
    - A. NKVD
    - *B. SAVAK
    - C. Cheka
    - D. okrana
    - E. Imam

16. The Khomeini movement is not only anti-Western, it is also
    - *A. antisemitic
    - B. anti-Islamic
    - C. anti-Parsee
    - D. anti-Shi'ite
    - E. antediluvian

17. The twelfth or hidden Imam is a tenet of the
    - A. Sunnis
    - B. Muslims
    - C. Parsees
    - *D. Shi'ites
    - E. Iraqis

18. In addition to affirmative and strategic elements, a modern revolutionary ideology involves
    - A. tactical elements
    - *B. critical elements
    - C. mythical elements
    - D. utopian elements
    - E. realistic elements

19. The revolutionary strategy associated with Mao Tse-tung is known as
    - *A. people's war
    - B. the guerrilla foco
    - C. conspiracy theory
    - D. the cultural revolution
    - E. the general strike

20. A catalytic approach to revolutionary leadership steers a middle course between mass-explosion and

A.   the great man theory   D.   spontaneous combustion
*B. conspiracy   E.   the Freudian approach
C.   the urban guerrilla theory

21. The pattern of change before a revolution is not only rapid, it is also
A.   antagonistic   D.   evolutionary
B.   dialectical   E.   incremental
*C. discordant

22. In addition to long-term and middle-term causes, a full picture of
revolutionary causation would include
A.   catalysts   D.   final causes
B.   sufficient causes   *E.   precipitants
C.   formal causes

23. RD, which figures in middle-term causes of revolution, means
A.   revolutionary determination D.   reactionary dilemma
B.   radical discontent   E.   retrograde disequilibrium
*C. relative deprivation

24. We owe the notion that revolutions exhibit three basic stages largely to
A.   Plato and Aristotle   D.   Trotsky and Stalin
*B. Edwards and Brinton   E.   Gilbert and Sullivan
C.   Marx and Engels

25. The winding-down of revolution is generally called
A.   the termination   D.   the status quo
B.   the adaptation   E.   the counterrevolution
*C. the Thermidor

Completion Questions

1. The actual emergence of a social movement comes in the ACTION stage and
its "structuralization of protest."

2. The prevalence of the administrator in the post-crisis stage of a social
movement worries the "old guard" of ideologists and AGITATORS.

3. The REVISIONIST approach to social movements endows them with largely
sociological features and a considerable amount of rationality.

4. Messianic movements are the chief form of MILLENARY movement.

5. The commune in South America where the Reverend Jim Jones and his
followers met their end was called JONESTOWN.

6. The "ideology" of the Jones movement was a strange mixture of Christian
fundamentalism and an offbeat sort of MARXISM.

7. The violence of a revolt is largely EXPRESSIVE.

8. Whatever his shortcomings, the Shah of Iran promoted MODERNIZATION even if in an erratic manner.

9. Though Muslims, Iranians are mostly of the minority sect of SHI'ITES.

10. Rather than to an Imam, the orthodox Sunni Muslims have historically looked to a CALIPH.

11. Instead of to Islamic themes, the Shah appealed to the myth of 2500 years of Iranian MONARCHY.

12. In Islam a *jihad* is a holy WAR.

13. The "king's-wicked-advisors" theory can justify a REVOLT, but not a revolution.

14. Secularization can undermine the RELIGIOUS aspect of a regime's legitimacy.

15. DEMOCRATIZATION means a leveling of social differences leading to revolutionary destabilization.

16. The alienation of INTELLECTUALS is an important middle-term cause of revolutions.

17. Abortive revolutions such as the Paris Commune of 1871 often follow MILITARY disasters.

18. When a number of middle-terms causes of revolution operate in a country, there exists a revolutionary SITUATION.

19. The storming of the Bastille on July 14, 1789 is a classic case of a PRECIPITANT of revolutions.

20. The rule of the MODERATES is considered by many the first phase of revolution.

21. The "Reign of Terror" is a term taken from the FRENCH revolution.

22. The radical phase of revolution is a clear dictatorship characterized by heightened political and economic CENTRALIZATION.

23. Sects of revolutionary purists, who accuse the radicals of betraying the revolution, are called ULTRAREVOLUTIONARIES.

24. One factor accounting for the winding down of revolution is the emergence of a new ELITE.

25. One reason for the strongly western orientation of the concept of revolution is the notion of PROGRESS it entails.

1. The broad long-term developments toward greater liberties and opportunities for women are a good example of a social movement. (F)

2. The incubation stage of a social movement is characterized by "structuralization of protest." (F)

3. Georges Sorel denied that a "utopian ideology" could inspire a vast mass movement, though it might do the trick with certain intellectuals. (T)

4. The dispute between the orthodox (Hoffer) and revisionist (Toch) views of social movements relates mainly to the problems of leadership. (F)

5. The Reverend Jim Jones was excommunicated from the Roman Catholic Church. (F)

6. With certain exceptions, we can say that youth movements fall on the left side of the political spectrum and nativistic movements on the right. (T)

7. A revolt is quite simply a revolution that did not get off the ground. (F)

8. Though most coups are clearly subrevolutionary, some can mark turning points between different phases of revolution. (T)

9. A single revolt may involve several distinct groups of protagonists. (T)

10. About half the world's Muslims are Shi'ites. (F)

11. The term "strategy" originated as an economic concept. (F)

12. It is necessary for all seven long-term causes of revolution to be active in order to produce a revolutionary situation. (F)

13. All revolutions go through three clear and distinct phases. (F)

14. Disunity is probably more lethal to a ruling class than incompetence. (T)

15. Revolutions generally involve a relaxation of moral rules and a freer and easier atmosphere. (F)

This chapter has two main concerns: (1) elaboration of a typology of competitive parties, followed by some analysis of structures and functions of political parties; and (2) analysis of the structure and some of the dynamics of two-party, moderate, and extreme multiparty systems. Two works are outstanding for this entire chapter: Duverger, Political Parties; and Sartori, Parties and Party Systems (see Suggestions). The Suggestions also refer to several anthologies with good contributions: LaPalombara and Wiener (especially the introduction and articles of Sartori and Daalder); Milnor (especially the Kirchheimer article); and Neumann (especially the introduction and the conclusion).

The first part of the chapter is clearly an elaboration of Duverger, plus Kirchheimer's concept of the "catchall" party. Some additional themes that might merit attention are (1) Anthony King's skeptical conclusions about the policy impact of parties and (2) whether the catchall party with its "pragmatism" and stress on consensus can grapple with the serious problems such as the "three Es"--economy, ecology, and energy.

Factions were (until recently) a rather ignored aspect of political life. Sartori's Parties and Party Systems, chapter 4, covers much of the theory. Case studies are found in F.P. Belloni and D.C. Beller, eds., Faction Politics: Political Parties and Factionalism in Comparative Perspective (Santa Barbara, Calif.: ABC-Clio, 1978).

On party systems, Duverger and Sartori are the best sources. The whole issue of the relationship between the electoral system, the party system, and political stability seems a "natural" for further discussion. See the Hermens' selection in D. Apter and H. Eckstein, eds., Comparative Politics (New York: Free Press, 1964), as well as Enid Lakeman, How Democracies Vote, and the relevant sections of Duverger and Sartori.

Multiple-Choice Questions

1. In early times the term "party" was synonymous with
   A. interest group   D. class
   *B. faction   E. movement
   C. cadre

2. Which of the following cannot be said of a cadre party?
   A. it appeals to the upper and middle classes
   B. leadership comes from the caucus
   C. finances come from a small number of big contributors
   *D. ideology is highly visible and highly structured
   E. extraparliamentary organization is rudimentary

3. Which of the following cannot be said of the mass party?
   *A. it is essentially an early nineteenth-century phenomenon
   B. it has a lower class orientation
   C. the early ones were strongly socialistic
   D. it has a bureaucratic hierarchy based on branches
   E. funds come from a large number of small contributors

4. To reach its goals of political education and organization the mass party
   sets up a number of
   A. plebiscites   D. political alliances
   *B. auxiliary organizations E. meetings
   C. interest groups

5. A good example of a French mass party is the
   A. Radical-Socialist party D. Independent party
   *B. Socialist party   E. Labor party
   C. Gaullist party

6. The thesis that the French, Italian, and other communist parties will
   respect constitutionalism is called
   A. Revisionism   D. Western Marxism
   B. polycentrism   E. the Historical Compromise
   *C. Eurocommunism

7. The Italian communist party
   A. is a member of recent cabinet coalitions
   B. has been declared illegal
   C. is the largest party in Italy
   *D. more or less supported the Government from 1976-79
   E. was pro-Chinese in the Sino-Soviet dispute

8. The basic goal of the catchall party is to
   A. nationalize private industry
   B. promote a strong ideology
   C. make members out of its voters
   *D. win elections
   E. cross the one-third barrier

9. A good German example of a party moving from a mass to a catchall party
   format is the
   A. Christian Democratic party   D. Social Democratic party
   B. Free Democratic party   E. Green party
   C. Nazi party

10. Members of a mass party who work extra hard for it are
    A. supporters   D. the inner circle
    B. candidate members   *E. militants
    C. true believers

11. The best definition of a party member is someone who
    A. votes consistently for it   D. campaigns for it
    *B. has formally joined it   E. joins its front organizations
    C. espouses its ideology

12. Besides ideology (and near-ideology), the nature of the times, and no
    issue content, voters are influenced by considerations of
    *A. group benefits   D. preferments
    B. patronage   E. personality traits
    C. economic interests

13. The function of political parties that synthesizes the diverse interests
    is called
    A. political socialization   D. functional alternatives
    B. system integration   E. interest articulation
    *C. interest aggregation

14. When we confront a "stable set of attitudes" instead of a "stable group
    of politicians" in a party, we are dealing with a(n)
    A. ideology   D. formation
    B. faction   *E. tendency
    C. conduit

15. Factionalism in the Israeli Labor party largely reflects
    A. disagreement over the Palestinian issue
    B. free enterprise versus socialism
    *C. that the party was once several parties
    D. Menachem Begin's leadership
    E. the peace treaty with Egypt

16. Who is not a former leader of the Israeli Labor party?
    A. David Ben-Gurion   *D. Rafi Haavoda
    B. Itzaak Rabin   E. Moshe Dayan
    C. Golda Meir

17. When political parties leave the center and cluster on the extreme left
    and right, we have
    *A. polarization   D. alternation
    B. agreement on fundamentals   E. ramification
    C. prevarication

18. The extreme multiparty system is associated with
    A. alternative governments   *D. marginal turnover

B. alternative coalitions   E. bogus coalition
C. grand coalition

19. The public opinion curve that seems essential to the two-party system is
 A. trimodal   D. nonmodal
*B. unimodal   E. multimodal
 C. bimodal

20. Sam Lubell characterized his American "moon" party as a
 A. party of propaganda   D. party of patronage
 B. party of decline   E. party of aspiration
*C. party of nostalgia

21. A recent development in Great Britain that could spell the passing of
the two-party system is the emergence of
 A. the National Front   D. trade union militancy
 B. the Falklands war   E. Welsh nationalism
*C. the Social Democratic party

22. In Scandinavia, the "bourgeois" parties include
 A. Liberals, Conservatives, and Social Democrats
 B. Liberals, Conservatives, and Communists
 C. Liberals, Social Democrats, and Communists
*D. Liberals, Conservatives, and Agrarians (Center)
 E. Liberals, Agrarians, and Farmers

23. Maurice Duverger advanced the controversial thesis that
 A. parties have little impact on policy
*B. the "center" is not a viable political force
 C. political ideals reflect economic realities
 D. PR is the "trojan horse" of democracy
 E. Eurocommunism is a fraud

24. In Fourth Republic France the "third force" was
 A. a renewal of the Popular Front of the Third Republic
 B. the bureaucracy that ruled because of parliamentary instability
*C. a coalition of centrist parties aligned against the right and left
 D. another name for the Socialist party
 E. the term for a neutralist foreign policy

25. When a party does not join the coalition cabinet but still votes for the
Government, we have a
 A. direct coalition   D. marginal coalition
*B. indirect coalition   E. grand coalition
 C. negative coalition

26. That the British Liberal party in 1929 got 23.5% of the popular vote,
but only 10% of the parliamentary seats is due to
 A. proportional representation   D. multiparty system
*B. single-member plurality system   E. the list system
 C. polarization

27. Which item below is incompatible with the list system?
 A. extreme multiparty system   D. preference vote
 B. relative majority   *E. single-member system
 C. moderate multiparty system

47

28. The most trenchant critic of PR is
    *A. F. A. Hermens   D. Max Weber
    B. Giovanni Sartori   E. Enid Lakeman
    C. Maurice Duverger

29. For many years the two largest West German parties have been
    A. FDP and CDU   *D. CDU and SPD
    B. SPD and FDP   E. NDP and SPD
    C. NDP and CDU

30. What Americans call a PAC West Germans call a
    A. single-issue group   D. social movement
    *B. citizens lobby   E. political party
    C. grass-roots movement

Completion Questions

1. While Edmund Burke stressed principles in his notion of party, Max Weber
    stressed POWER.

2. MASS parties were a political response to a broadened suffrage.

3. President MITTERRAND of France was a key force in the resurgence of the
    Socialist party.

4. The most elementary unit of a communist party is the CELL.

5. In 1981 the French president called the COMMUNISTS into the government
    for the first time in over three decades.

6. The CATCHALL party tries to appeal to the maximum number of social groups
    with almost no exceptions.

7. "True believers" and "careerists" are two types of party MILITANT.

8. A FRONT organization is set up when a party wants to conceal its real
    involvement.

9. The political SOCIALIZATION role of parties involves the inculcation of
    the fundamental values and norms of the system.

10. Catchall parties are perhaps the best suited to perform the function of
    interest AGGREGATION.

11. Political parties can serve as a dual channel of COMMUNICATION.

12. A policy faction in a political party is based on either IDEOLOGY or
    strategy.

13. The present Israeli Labor party dates only from 1968.

14. Ideology, personality, and AGE are causes of factionalism in the Israeli Labor party.

15. Ideological DISTANCE measures how far apart are the extreme left and extreme right parties.

16. In the extreme multiparty system an extremist DRIVE pushes nearly all parties further either to the right or to the left.

17. Sam Lubell's SUN party in American politics is so strong because it appeals to social groups on the rise.

18. The third largest vote-getting party in Great Britain today is the LIBERAL party.

19. Scandinavia represents a MODERATE multiparty system.

20. In recent years the Swedish Social Democrats have been in a coalition with the COMMUNIST party.

21. In an extreme multiparty only a few parties have COALITION potential because of overall support for the existing system.

22. As the minority Labor Government in 1924 depended on the Liberal party for votes in parliament, it is a case of INDIRECT coalition.

23. According to F. A. Hermens a multiparty system leads directly to political INSTABILITY and then to breakdown of the system.

24. Defenders of PR maintain that this electoral system may reflect deep-seated social CLEAVAGES more than produce them.

25. West Germany elects the Bundestag half by PR and half by SINGLE-MEMBER constituencies.

True-False Questions

1. Full-fledged political parties have marked the politics of all historical civilizations as far back as classical antiquity. (F)

2. The sketchy organization and vague ideology of the cadre party is mainly due to the restricted electorate at the time of its prevalence. (T)

3. Ideology is used for political mobilization, which has been the prime task of catchall parties. (F)

4. Clearly the Communists have superseded the Socialists as the dominant force on the French left for some years to come. (F)

5. The recent inclusion of Communists in the Italian cabinet marks their return there after nearly forty years in the political wilderness. (F)

6. A catchall party will tend to move toward the center of the ideological spectrum. (T)

7. A sympathizer is a member of a party who does not choose to be very active in its behalf. (F)

8. If an English businessman votes for the Conservative party because he feels that that party helps businessmen like himself, his basic motivation reflects "the nature of the times." (F)

9. An exceptionally good case of a party delivering on its policy promises was the Labor Government in Great Britain in 1924. (F)

10. Economic factions in political parties are based on large outside interest groups such as trade unions and farmers organizations. (T)

11. The basic contrast among party systems runs between the two-party and moderate multiparty systems on the one hand and the extreme multiparty system on the other. (T)

12. The routs of Barry Goldwater in 1964 and George McGovern in 1972 are due at least in part to the bimodal distribution of opinion in the United States. (F)

13. The Swedish Social Democrats and the Norwegian Labor party are basically similar parties playing a similar role in similar types of party systems. (T)

14. In terms of simple fairness, the single-member plurality system is inferior to PR. (T)

15. The evolution of the West German party system suggests that PR, when limited and qualified, does not necessarily lead to an extreme multiparty system. (T)

This chapter deals with four basic themes: (1) a survey of typologies of interest groups, (2) examination of the key modes of interest-group access to the political system with special reference to the notion of corporatism, (3) an exploration of the nature of public opinion, and (4) a look at the techniques of political propaganda.   The whole chapter is influenced by David B. Truman's The Governmental Process.

On typologies of interest groups, Almond's is widely used in the literature.   But since most work is done on the association, the typology based on Meynaud seems more refined.   Some general points that might be covered in lectures include (1) how parties differ from interest groups and (2) whether the present geographical system of representation should be replaced by the direct representation of interest groups, i.e., so-called economic parliaments.   Hayward's book cited in fn. 20 on the French Economic and Social Council might be helpful.   Some lecture discussion of the problem of corporatism would do well to look to the April 1977 issue of Comparative Political Studies, which is entirely devoted to the problem.   For case-study materials see fn. 44 in the text.

Regarding access, in addition to Truman's book the "case studies" of Stewart, LaPalombara, and Braunthal provide good comparative information.

With respect to public opinion and propaganda, the treatment in Truman has held up remarkably well.   Also useful are the books by Key, Rosenau, and Lippmann cited in the Suggestions.   For a study of elite (parliamentary) opinion in Great Britain and Italy, see Roger D. Putnam, The Beliefs of Politicians (New Haven: Yale University Press, 1973.)   Also see Ronald Inslehart, The Silent Revolution (Princeton: Princeton University Press, 1977) for a study of changes in Western public opinion.

1. In David Truman's classic formulation, what distinguishes interest groups
    from casual formations or statistical categories of people is
    A.   political activity   D.   latency
    B.   party affiliation   *E.   shared attitudes
    C.   bureaucratic organization

2. Along with associational and nonassociational interest groups, Gabriel
    Almond's typology includes
    A.   latent and manifest groups
    B.   partisan and nonpartisan groups
    *C. anomic and institutional groups
    D.   formal and informal groups
    E.   ethnic and religious groups

3. The apex of a federally-structured interest association is called a(n)
    A.   auxiliary organization   D.   quasi-group
    *B. peak association   E.   international
    C.   confederation

4. The three main types of pressure group are the business-institutional,
    category-defense, and
    A.   citizens lobbies   D.   propaganda groups
    B.   public interest groups   E.   multinationals
    *C. promotional groups

5. The Federation of German Industries (BDI) is
    A.   the largest German trade union
    *B. generally favorable to the Christian Democrats and Free Democrats
    C.   absolutely neutral in politics
    D.   a business-institutional pressure group
    E.   the parent company of Volkswagen

6. The ability of an interest group to reach important centers of political
    decision is known as
    A.   intermediation   D.   output
    B.   intervention   *E.   access
    C.   aggregation

7. When a government agency considers a group "the natural expression and
    representative of a given social sector," we have a
    A.   symbiotic relationship   D.   manifest relationship
    *B. clientele relationship   E.   preferential relationship
    C.   dominance relationship

8. The French consultative body that groups two hundred members from
    business, labor, farmers, and other organizations is the
    A.   Council of State
    B.   Senate
    *C. Economic and Social Council
    D.   General Confederation of Labor
    E.   National Council of Corporations

9. Lobbying
    A. always employs corrupt and questionable techniques
    B. means any attempt to exert personal influence
    *C. classically involves the attempt to influence legislation
    D. is illegal in the United States
    E. originally referred to litigation

10. Personal lobbying involves techniques like the mass assault, the steady trickle, and the
    A. confrontation   *D. deputation
    B. manifestation   E. coup de main
    C. contestation

11. One thing that distinguishes an alliance from simple log-rolling is
    A. legality   D. secrecy
    B. executive intervention E. none of the above
    *C. the scope of the relationship

12. Litigation means
    A. bribery   D. pork-barrel legislation
    B. collusion   *E. going to court
    C. malfeasance

13. What the Italians call "parentela" means that an interest group
    A. is fully neutral toward all parties
    B. shifts its support from party to party
    *C. selects one party as its "own"
    D. forms its own party
    E. is completely dominated by a party

14. Opinion-holders are divided into the very large mass public and the very small
    A. phantom public   *D. attentive public
    B. opinion makers   E. intellectual elite
    C. dynamic public

15. Which of the following is not true about mass public opinion?
    A. the level of information on issues is low
    B. the views involved are rather opaque and incoherent
    *C. it is relatively inconsequential in political life
    D. the level of ideology is low
    E. it is subject to rapid changes of mood

16. The most difficult goal of the propagandist is
    A. specific propaganda
    *B. changing attitudes
    C. stimulating favorable preexisting attitudes
    D. reducing cognitive dissonance
    E. utilizing the mass media

17. The "target" group of propaganda is
    A. the group employing the propagandist
    B. the group the propagandist seeks to discredit

C. the group the propagandist wants to glorify
*D. the group the propagandist seeks to reach
E. the group that eludes the propagandist's manipulation

18. Walter Lippmann found the most serious obstacles to the propagandist's hope to change attitudes lie in
    A. preconceptions   D. complexes
    B. attitudes   E. interests
    *C. stereotypes

19. When the propagandist omits qualifying if not contradictory information from his message, we have
    *A. gross oversimplification   D. manifest rejection
    B. subliminal conditioning   E. partial projection
    C. selective perception

20. Because the propagandist cannot always penetrate into the minds of those he wishes to influence, we can speak of a
    A. brainwashing   D. mind-set
    *B. perceptual screen   E. predispositional faculty
    C. cognitive limitation

21. The notion of corporatism demands a rejection or revision of which general theory of politics?
    *A. pluralism   D. individualism
    B. collectivism   E. polycentrism
    C. syndicalism

22. In a corporatist system, in exchange for official recognition and privileged position the leaders of interest associations pay the price of
    A. campaign contributions
    *B. compliance with government policy
    C. "under-the-table" payoffs
    D. conflict of interest penalties
    E. none of the above

23. In the Mexican version of corporatism
    A. the PRI penetrates all corporatist policymaking
    B. we have "state corporatism" similar to Fascist Italy
    C. the system is strengthened through a figurehead presidency
    *D. big business is a prime beneficiary
    E. farmers are completely out of the system

24. In Mexican labor relations
    A. workers are not part of the corporatist system
    *B. the strike is basically inoperative
    C. workers are represented in CONCANACO and CONCAMIN
    D. the PRI is wholly excluded
    E. none of the above

25. The type of planning used in France is
    A. imperative planning   D. collectivist planning
    *B. indicative planning   E. comprehensive planning
    C. socialist planning

26. Which of the following historical points has not contributed to the strength and character of French corporatism?
    A. poor economic performance   *D. consumerism
    B. statism   E. none of the above
    C. technocracy

27. French corporatist-style economic planning involved the close working relationship between higher civil servants and
    A. trade union leaders   D. mass media leaders
    *B. big business leaders   E. the Socialist party
    C. parliamentary politicians

Completion Questions

1. ANOMIC interest groups are "more or less spontaneous penetrations into the political system . . . such as riots, demonstrations, assassinations and the like."

2. Unions, farmers organizations, veterans groups, trade associations, professional and other groups are examples of CATEGORY-defense pressure groups.

3. Since the end of World War II the Italian Catholic Action has been associated with the CHRISTIAN DEMOCRATIC party.

4. Because of the transformation of parliamentarism no pressure group can afford to ignore the PREPARLIAMENTARY stage of policy.

5. Bribery can be a technique of LOBBYING.

6. In West Germany so-called "sponsors organizations" act as intermediaries between PARTIES and individual business firms.

7. In the United States log-rolling is quite often used with PORK BARREL legislation.

8. With postparliamentary access, actual policy implementation and amplification of statutes is left to special bureaus and REGULATORY commissions.

9. The Poujadiste party of the closing days of the Fourth French Republic originated as a PRESSURE-GROUP.

10. The MASS public may include more than 90 percent of the population.

11. Intellectuals would generally be considered members of the ATTENTIVE public.

12. To make sure that people receive his message the propagandist often resorts to attention-getting SYMBOLS.

13. REPETITION, perhaps the simplest propaganda technique, may work by leaving a subliminal residue in people's mind.

14. To equate the welfare state with socialism or even communism illustrates the propaganda technique of gross OVERSIMPLIFICATION.

15. PLURALISM is the theory that most closely relates public policy to the activity of interest groups.

16. In the corporatist approach the STATE becomes more autonomous and activist, while the interest groups become more controlled and passive.

17. In a corporatist system certain special interest associations are given a virtual monopoly of representation for special sectors of the ECONOMY.

18. In contrast to state corporatism, SOCIETAL corporatism means that functional groups are not brought whole cloth into the government organization.

19. The Mexican Constitution of 1917 contains not only reformist, but even SOCIALISTIC goals.

20. For historical reasons the corporatist relationship of government and BUSINESS takes place largely outside the single-party (PRI).

21. Workers and peasants were the supposed beneficiaries of the Mexican REVOLUTION of 1910.

22. The Mexican ejidatarios are PEASANTS.

23. French TECHNOCRACY means that "progress can be achieved by the 'depoliticization' of problems."

24. Corporatist-style planning in France occurred largely without the cooperation of the UNIONS.

25. The NIXON Administration in the United States took some steps toward corporatist policymaking with the institution of a wage-price stabilization board.

True-False Questions

1. Institutions are the prevalent form of interest group in politics of modern societies. (F)

2. Indirect access involves the mediatory role of legislators, bureaucrats, and judges. (F)

3. The French Economic and Social Council illustrates the politics of consultation. (T)

4. Lobbying is originally a British expression. (F)

5. In Great Britain as elsewhere it is unlawful for M.P.'s to accept retainers from outside organizations. (F)

6. In both France and Italy the main trade unions have overcome past political divisions to work for common economic goals. (T)

7. Pluralists tend to view political parties as coalitions of interest groups. (T)

8. When an interest group "shops around" for suitable candidates and parties to support, this means that ideology prevails over pragmatic considerations. (F)

9. Members of the attentive public tend to be more ideological than members of the mass public. (T)

10. In some ways public opinion is becoming a more formidable force than in the past. (T)

11. Specific propaganda builds up a reservoir of "good will" that can be tapped at some future date. (F)

12. Attention-getting symbols may or may not have something to do with the content of the propagandist's message. (T)

13. In Mexican corporatism the workers and peasants organization relate to the state through the medium of the ruling party the PRI. (T)

14. The coming to power of President Mitterrand and the Socialists in 1981 has weakened still further the French Government's commitment to economic planning. (F)

15. Parties, parliaments, and public opinion--important aspects of the theory and practice of modern democracy--are largely left out in the cold in extreme forms of corporatist policymaking. (T)

Chapter 9: Ideology and Political Culture

This chapter has two main concerns: (1) the elaboration of a tight concept of ideology that stresses its independent political role, and (2) an exposition of the more diffuse notions of political culture and subculture.

On ideology, Waxman's The End of Ideology Debate not only rehearses the specific debate of the title, but also gives good examples of the contrast between loose and tight definitions of ideology. Mannheim's Ideology and Utopia retains its seminal quality after many years.

On political culture, The Civic Culture and The Civic Culture Revisited (see Suggestions) are important, though the conceptual framework seems beyond the introductory level. Nonetheless, both books contain descriptive materials on the United States, Great Britain, West Germany, Italy, and Mexico. A less technical approach is found in Walter A. Rosenbaum, Political Culture (New York: Praeger, 1975); eminently relevant remains Lipset's Political Man.

On subcultures, Lijphart's Democracy in Plural Societies explicates and exemplifies the consociational democracy theme. See notes 13 and 19 in the text for more on the Netherlands and Lebanon.

For political socialization, see Kenneth P. Langton, Political Socialization (New York: Oxford University Press, 1969) for a standard account, and the anthology gathered by Roberta Sigel, Learning About Politics (New York: Random House, 1970). Also see Charles G. Bell's collection, Growth and Change (Encino, Calif.: Dickenson, 1973).

Multiple-Choice Questions

1. A tight conception of ideology stresses such elements as
   *A. program, rhetoric, philosophy, and strategy
   B. beliefs, values, norms
   C. beliefs, tactics, strategy, philosophy
   D. strategy, tactics, objectives
   E. strategy, norms, worldview

2. Romanticism stresses the primacy of
   A. reason   D. irrationality
   B. freedom   *E. feeling
   C. strategy

3. Which ideological function answers the question: "Why does the group in power have legitimacy?"
   A. mystification   D. mobilization
   B. obfuscation   E. ossification
   *C. justification

4. The contrast between esoteric and exoteric ideology regards
   A. general versus specific principles
   B. abstract versus concrete elements
   C. philosophical versus strategic elements
   D. value-free versus value-laden elements
   *E. elite and mass levels of ideology

5. There is a basically symbiotic relationship between ideology and
   A. philosophy   D. belief systems
   *B. political practice   E. movements
   C. institutions

6. The contrast to preformed ideology is
   A. exoteric ideology   D. tight ideology
   B. preformed ideology   E. latent ideology
   *C. ad hoc ideology

7. Fidel Castro somewhat belatedly proclaimed himself a(n)
   A. ideologist   D. Realpolitiker
   B. Fascist   *E. Marxist-Leninist
   C. nationalist

8. In contemporary political science the notion of political culture has more or less replaced the older notion of
   A. ideology   D. social tradition
   *B. national character   E. Weltanschauung
   C. power politics

9. For a long while "modernization" was equated with
   A. democracy   D. political culture
   B. communism   E. technology
   *C. westernization

10. A country's political culture is really the cluster of its political
    A. parties   *D. subcultures
    B. behavior   E. pluralism
    C. ideologies

11. One method of acknowledging the diversity of plural societies is
    A. the single-member system   D. pluralistic democracy
    B. a plural executive   E. homogenization
    *C. a federal system

12. One element of the formula of consociational democracy is
    *A. a grand coalition   D. minority governments
    B. parallel convergence   E. alternative governments
    C. a plural executive

13. Consociational democracy more or less implements John C. Calhoun's
    principle of the
    A. numerical majority   D. dissident majority
    *B. concurrent majority   E. errant majority
    C. relative majority

14. The largest religious group in the Netherlands is the
    *A. Roman Catholics   D. Protestants
    B. Calvinists   E. Jews
    C. seculars

15. Seculars in the Netherlands are split between the liberal bloc and the
    A. humanist bloc   D. unaffiliated bloc
    B. agnostic bloc   E. communist bloc
    *C. socialist bloc

16. Which of the following was not one of the "big five" parties generally
    found in Dutch governments from 1945 to 1965?
    A. Catholic Peoples party   D. the Labor Party
    B. the Christian Historical Union *E. the Farmers party
    C. the Anti-Revolutionary party

17. The Christian Democratic Appeal founded in 1976 in the Netherlands joins
    which two parties to the Catholic Peoples party?
    A. the Antirevolutionaries and the Labor party
    B. the Antirevolutionaries and the Reformed Political League
    *C. the Antirevolutionaries and the Christian Historicals
    D. the Antirevolutionaries and the Roman Catholic party
    E. the Political Reformed League and the Political Reformed party

18. Recent Dutch electoral trends suggest
    A. an Italianization of the party system
    *B. a Germanization of the party system
    C. an Americanization of the party system
    D. an Anglicization of the party system
    E. a Lebanonization of the party system

19. Under Ottoman imperial administration the "millet" system allowed
    religious communities a strong measure of

        A. toleration   D. conflict
        B. tribute   E. intermarriage
      *C. self-government

20. The most European-oriented of Lebanon's religious blocs are the
        A. Greek Catholics   D. Druze
      *B. Maronites   E. Phalangists
        C. Greek Orthodox

21. The Mufti of the Republic is the head of Lebanon's
        A. Maronites   D. Shi'ites
      *B. Sunnis   E. Greek Catholics
        C. Druzes

22. According to the National Pact the Lebanese president must be a
        A. Muslim   *D. Maronite
        B. Greek   E. Druze
        C. Christian

23. In addition to regular political parties the Lebanese parliament contains
        A. interest groups   D. splinter parties
        B. religious communities   E. social movements
      *C. personal blocs

24. The two chief schools of thought about political socialization are the
     Freudians and the
        A. Jungians   D. behaviorists
      *B. developmentalists   E. Eriksonians
        C. Marxists

25. In totalitarian systems political socialization takes the form of
        A. development   D. brainwashing
        B. enculturation   E. sensitivity
      *C. indoctrination

26. The Authoritarian Personality (1950) studied in part
      *A. fascistic personality   D. totalitarian personality
        B. communist personality   E. Hitler, Stalin, Robespierre
        C. psychology of leadership

27. The relationship of teachers to pupils involves
      *A. latent political socialization
        B. the authoritarian personality
        C. ad hoc political socialization
        D. manifest political socialization
        E. quasi-socialization

28. What has traditionally been considered the strongest influence on
     political socialization?
        A. the peer group   *D. the family
        B. the workplace   E. the school
        C. the church

29. The theory that suggests that pragmatic "bread-and-butter" issues have

superseded profound conflicts of principle is called

*A. the end of ideology   D. power politics
 B. economic determinism   E. the welfare state
 C. the agonizing reappraisal

30. A movement of the 1960s that suggested that ideology was alive and well
    in the western world was
    A. the New Right   D. consumerism
    B. environmentalism   E. neoconservatism
   *C. the New Left

Completion Questions

1. Loose conceptions of ideology equate it with BELIEF system.

2. INTELLECTUALS have a special disposition toward ideologies and are the
   leading edge of the attentive public.

3. ROMANTICISM is a doctrine that stresses feeling over reason.

4. Rhetoric is the art of PERSUASION.

5. The rhetorical element of ideology suggests an appeal to human EMOTION.

6. The justification function of ideologies corresponds to Gaetano Mosca's
   notion of the political FORMULA.

7. Ideologies MOBILIZE by playing on the hopes and fears of regime or
   movement followers.

8. ESOTERIC ideology is the level of ideology that requires study and
   meditation.

9. EXOTERIC ideology is likely to blame scapegoats for the troubles of a
   given group.

10. All politically successful regimes deviate somewhat from their PREFORMED
    ideology, if indeed they have one.

11. REGIONAL subcultures derive from ecologically distinct parts of the
    country.

12. PILLARS is a peculiarly Dutch term for the phenomenon of subcultural
    blocs.

13. The four elements of the formula of consociational democracy are grand
    coalition, mutual veto, autonomy, and PROPORTIONALITY.

14. For a long time Dutch patriotism seemed synonymous with CALVINIST
    protestantism.

15. For most of this century the PARTIES were the "central and most inclusive agencies" of Dutch subcultural blocs.

16. The Dutch Communists, Pacifist-Socialists, and Democratic Socialists '70 could be considered spin-offs from the SOCIALIST bloc.

17. The States General is the Dutch PARLIAMENT.

18. The recent merger of the three large religious parties in the Netherlands resulted in the Christian Democratic APPEAL.

19. From 1920 to 1943 Lebanon was under a FRENCH mandate.

20. Lebanese Maronites, Greek Orthodox, and Greek Catholics are each led by a PATRIARCH.

21. According to the National Pact of 1943 the speaker of the Lebanese parliament must be a SHI'ITE.

22. The stronger Lebanese parties possess their own PARAMILITARY units.

23. Freudian approaches to political personality stress the crucial role of the OEDIPUS complex.

24. The PEER group is the individual's circle of friends and acquaintances.

25. End-of-ideology theorists maintained that INTELLECTUALS had learned some bitter lessons form the course of modern history.

True-False Questions

1. One inference from a tight definition of ideology is that both the attentive and the mass public will be pervaded by ideology. (F)

2. A political ideology can be considered a grandiose philosophical system. (F)

3. Rationalism undergirded many ideologies of the eighteenth-century enlightenment. (T)

4. Both Nazism and the American New Left were influenced by themes of romanticist thought. (T)

5. Rhetoric is the science of right reasoning and employs the syllogism both to conclude and to convince. (F)

6. Only the extremist ideologies of the right and the left perform the function of justification. (F)

7. The ideologist always sees things in politics less clearly than the non-ideologist. (F)

8. Condorcet, an eighteenth-century French political philosopher, suggested that political institutions work best where the political culture is such to support them. (F)

9. Political culture is a more inclusive notion than ideology. (T)

10. The two-party system seems especially appropriate for a consociational democracy. (F)

11. Historically speaking, age subcultures are less frequent and politically salient than most other types of subculture. (T)

12. The "plural" quality of Dutch society has been declining in recent years. (T)

13. The Dutch Radical party was basically a group of disgruntled right-wing protestants. (F)

14. Lebanese consociationalism might have survived were it not for the impact of external political factors. (T)

15. The bloc aspect of the Lebanese political culture is stronger than that of the Netherlands. (T)

This chapter concentrates on five polyvalent themes--progress/utopia, democracy, freedom, socialism, and nationalism--that more or less cut across the left-right ideological spectrum. They are crosscutting because they appear in several of the nine ideological systems covered in chapter 11. They are polyvalent because they mean different, sometimes radically different, things to different people. The text strives not only to give students some flavoring of alternative ideological usages of the five themes but also to point to some bedrock meanings for each. The difference from other texts is seen in that the others generally consider democracy, socialism, and nationalism to be pure and simple ideologies. Here we prefer to consider them themes because of their diverse and shifting meanings. Naturally the text has only scratched the surface of these exceedingly rich and complex themes, and the instructor may feel that any or all deserve class reinforcement or expansion.

On the notion of progress, the books by Bury and Nisbet in the Suggestions are essential. For utopias, the histories by Mumford and the Manuels provide good background.

On democracy, the anthology edited by Kariel (see Suggestions) gives a good representation of divergent primary sources. On the monographic level, the books by Dahl, Bachrach, Sartori, and Spitz are at least minor classics.

On freedom, Isaiah Berlin's Two Concepts of Liberty (see Suggestions) is fundamental.

For socialism, Berki's book shows different emphases in the socialist tradition. The same comes out in the fine anthology edited by Irving Howe, Essential Works of Socialism (New York: Bantam Books, 1971). Because the text asserts that socialism must be understood in contrast to capitalism, Andrew Shonfield's Modern Capitalism (New York: Oxford University Press, 1976; originally published in 1965) is a fine source.

On nationalism, the books by Smith and Davis (see Suggestions) are quite helpful, especially the former. Also the classic studies of Hans Kohn, The Idea of Nationalism (New York: Macmillan, 1961), and E.H. Carr, Nationalism and After (London: Macmillan, 1945) give a good historical survey of nationalism.

1. As a political concept, progress means a change over time that produces
    an increase in
    A. happiness   D. justice
    *B. value   E. development
    C. technology

2. The German philosopher Hegel envisaged progress largely as the growth of
    A. technology   D. democracy
    B. classes   E. religion
    *C. freedom

3. The person who coined the term "utopia" was
    A. Plato   D. Tomasso Campanella
    *B. Sir Thomas More   E. Hegel
    C. Karl Marx

4. Most utopias hope to eradicate all but which of the following?
    A. poverty   D. exploitation
    B. crime   *E. elites
    C. social conflict

5. Utopias of abundance stand in sharp contrast to utopias of
    A. reconstruction   D. socialism
    B. escape   E. conservatives
    *C. frugality

6. Societal democracy preaches general equality of
    A. power   *D. condition
    B. elites   E. stabilization
    C. freedom

7. The "demos" of the word democracy stands for
    A. to rule   D. state
    B. majority   E. the poor
    *C. the people

8. Which of the following most direcly reflects the notion of pure or direct
    democracy?
    A. the United States House of Representatives
    B. the United States Supreme Court
    Ç. the Masschusetts House of Representatives
    D. the Federal bureaucracy
    *E. the New England town meeting

9. The major proponent of the idea of the discreet representative was
    A. John Locke   D. Rousseau
    B. Montesquieu   E. Plato
    *C. Edmund Burke

10. Which of the following best embodies the mandated delegate principle?

66

A. the British House of Commons
B. the British House of Lords
C. the United States Supreme Court
*D. the United Nations General Assembly
E. the French Council of State

11. Individualist democracy can also be termed
    A. collectivist democracy   D. mass democracy
    *B. liberal democracy   E. pure democracy
    C. societal democracy

12. Some modern theories of democracy subscribe to Bentham's principle of
    A. the general will
    B. the mandated delegate
    *C. the greatest happiness of the greatest number
    D. collectivism
    E. pluralism

13. Rousseau's chief contribution to democratic theory involves his notion of
    A. utility   *D. the general will
    B. minority rights   E. elites
    C. the discreet representative

14. The term most closely associated with Roberto Michels's attack on classic
    democratic theory is
    A. particular will   D. elite
    *B. oligarchy   E. ochlocracy
    C. ruling class

15. For Joseph Schumpeter the chief weakness of classic democratic theory
    concerned
    A. representation   D. the public interest
    B. minority rights   E. economics
    *C. leadership

16. In stark contrast to classic democratic theory, democratic elitism sees
    positive benefits to the system in
    A. elites   *D. apathy
    B. dictatorship   E. alienation
    C. mandated delegates

17. In recent years democratic elitism has been criticized for
    underestimating the importance of
    A. representation   D. politicization
    B. elites   E. mobilization
    *C. participation

18. Negative freedom suggests an absence of
    A. freedom   D. the state
    B. justice   E. mind
    *C. restraints

19. Which of the following comes closest to a negative notion of freedom?
    A. Rousseau   D. Hegel

    B. John Dewey   *E. John Stuart Mill
    C. Karl Marx

20. Positive freedom most closely suggests
    A. unimpeded movement   D. equality of condition
    B. anarchistic individualism   E. other-regarding actions
    *C. moral development

21. For Hegel freedom is closely associated with
    A. equality   D. religion
    *B. the state   E. the general will
    C. socialism

22. The core idea of socialism involves
    A. indicative planning   D. religion
    *B. public ownership   E. utopianism
    C. human brotherhood

23. Which of the following is not associated with imperative planning?
    A. collectivist planning   D. the force of law
    *B. Yugoslav socialism   E. bureaucracy
    C. centralization

24. Both anarchosyndicalism and guild socialism stress
    *A. trade unions   D. bureaucracy
    B. a central planning board   E. disaggregation
    C. private enterprise

25. The Russiam anarchists Bakunin and Kropotkin advocated
    A. anarchosyndicalism   D. guilds
    B. bureaucracy   E. a command economy
    *C. localist socialism

26. For ultimate communism Karl Marx advocated the rule "from each
    according to his ability, to each according to his
    A. class   D. taste
    *B. needs   E. ability
    C. work

27. When it comes to movements, it is important to distinguish nationalism
    from
    A. patriotism   D. nativism
    B. ethnocentrism   E. tribalism
    *C. national sentiment

28. Zionism could be considered a(n)
    A. fragment movement   D. irredentist movement
    B. secessionist movement   *E. diaspora movement
    C. mixed movement

29. A nationalist movement that longs after one big nation composed of
    diverse states and peoples is a(n)
    A. territorial movement   D. ethnic movement
    *B. pan-movement   E. irredentist movement
    C. mixed movement

30. Which group was excluded from the nation by certain ideologists of the
    French Revolution?
    A. the clergy   D. the Gallo-Romans
    *B. the nobility   E. the third estate
    C. the bourgeoisie

Completion Questions

1. Theories of progress are either INFINITE or plateau theories.

2. Theories of progress are either unilinear or WAVELIKE.

3. Utopias are either "utopias of escape" or utopias of RECONSTRUCTION.

4. Utopians tend to have an optimistic or plastic view of human NATURE.

5. In utopias politics is to be replaced by ADMINISTRATION.

6. Karl Marx coined the expression "utopian SOCIALISM" to criticize
    reformers who thought their utopian projects made revolution unnecessary.

7. Edmund Burke rejected the mandated delegate theory of representation
    because the true representative's duty was to search for a single
    NATIONAL interest.

8. In classic liberal democracy "society" is a name for INDIVIDUALS who make
    it up.

9. In Rousseau's teaching, at the national level the will of ALL is the
    unethical counterpart to the ethical general will.

10. Rousseau's idea that the minority "must be forced to be FREE" alarms some
    liberals and individualists.

11. All forms of classic democratic theory involve the principles of majority
    rule, political equality, and PARTICIPATION of all citizens.

12. While traditional antidemocratic thought considered democracy to be
    undesirable, classic elitism considered it rather to be IMPOSSIBLE.

13. In democratic elitism, democracy is seen as a kind of marketplace, where
    competing ELITES display they wares to the consuming public.

14. Democratic elitists sometimes view low levels of political participation
    as a kind of vote of CONFIDENCE in the system.

15. The "politics of confrontation" is sometimes favored by advocates of
    PARTICIPATORY democracy.

16. John Stuart Mill's view of freedom is premised upon the contrast between self-regarding and other-regarding <u>ACTIONS</u>.

17. In individualistic theories of positive freedom, there is usually a dichotomy between our higher and our lower <u>SELVES</u>.

18. Modern liberalism fears that doing too much to help the individual results in social <u>PATERNALISM</u>.

19. In many respects the natural opposite of socialism is <u>CAPITALISM</u>.

20. Collectivist socialism would find the central planning board giving small portions of the national plan to various national <u>MINISTRIES</u>.

21. The two types of decentralization compatible with collectivist socialism are at the enterprise and the <u>REGIONAL</u> level.

22. The trade unions are the darling of both varieties of <u>FUNCTIONAL</u> socialism.

23. Guild socialism differs from anarchosyndicalism because it allows for the survival of the <u>STATE</u>.

24. Early socialist doctrines stressed <u>DISTRIBUTION</u> far more than production.

25. Governments today often use fiscal and <u>MONETARY</u> policy to direct the economy in socially desirable directions.

26. <u>INDICATIVE</u> planning is far less comprehensive and compulsory than imperative planning.

27. <u>NATION-BUILDING</u> is the attempt to weld together a population divided by primordial sentiments of race, religion, region, or tribe.

28. In Anthony Smith's "core nationalist doctrine," nations are a <u>NATURAL</u> division of mankind.

29. An ethnic nationalist movement in a multinational empire is generally a <u>SECESSIONIST</u> movement.

30. At various times Chairman Mao appealed to <u>IDEOLOGY</u> to define the membership of classes in the Chinese nation.

True-False Questions

1. Theories of progress and utopian projects both preach the boundless perfectability of mankind. (F)

2. The idea of progress is so flexible that it figures both in status quo and radical ideologies. (T)

3. Some utopias of escape are presented seriously as blueprints for the future of mankind. (F)

4. All utopias are fundamentally egalitarian. (F)

5. For centuries theorists figured that democracy was appropriate only for small or tiny states. (T)

6. The Burkean theory of the discreet representative has clearly won out over the mandated delegate theory. (F)

7. Both individualist and collectivist democracy justify majority rule on the same grounds. (F)

8. Rousseau called the identification of the objective public interest with the individual's interest "the general will." (T)

9. Of the classic elitists, Michels ended up as the most favorable toward democracy. (F)

10. John Dewey was in many respects a precursor of recent theories of participatory democracy. (T)

11. Theories of positive freedom maintain that a simple absence of restraints or restrictions can degenerate into mere license. (T)

12. The best historical examples of functional socialism are found in the Soviet Union and other communist regimes. (F)

13. G. D. H. Cole was the chief theorist of guild socialism. (T)

14. Nationalism is an ideology. (F)

15. Pan-movements and diaspora movements have in common the desire to reunite what has been rent asunder. (T)

Chapter 11: The Left-Right Ideological Spectrum

Consulting the Suggestions and chapter footnotes should provide ample
background materials for the various standpoints on the ideological spectrum.

1. The origin of the terms "left" and "right" has to do with
   A. Parisian river banks
   *B. a seating arrangement
   C. a plan of battle
   D. a famous painting
   E. the columns of a book

2. Which term best approximates the literal meaning of "anarchy"?
   A. chaos
   B. state of nature
   *C. no rule
   D. tyranny
   E. mob-rule

3. Perhaps the most radical of the individualistic anarchists was
   A. Michael Bakunin
   B. Peter Kropotkin
   C. Georges Sorel
   *D. Max Stirner
   E. Immanuel Kant

4. Anarchists disagree most emphatically with Marxists on the role of the
   A. revolution
   *B. state
   C. church
   D. bourgeoisie
   E. individual

5. Among the formative influences upon Karl Marx are French socialism, German philosophy, and
   A. Italian elitism
   B. American technology
   C. Austrian economics
   D. Scandinavian social democracy
   *E. British political economy

6. Karl Marx absorbed much of his dialectical method from
   A. David Ricardo
   B. Immanual Kant
   C. Robert Paul Wolff
   *D. G. W. F. Hegel
   E. Friedrich Engels

7. The critical transition in a dialectical pattern of change is the
   A. crucial point
   B. point of no return
   C. counterpoint
   *D. nodal point
   E. threshhold factor

8. Which of the following is not included in Marx's "superstructure"?
   A. the state
   B. ideology
   *C. mode of production
   D. religion
   E. law

9. What did Marx see as the ultimate motive force of history?
   A. ideas
   B. ideology
   *C. technology
   D. interests
   E. mind

10. Which of the following is not a stage in Marx's view of world history?
    A. capitalism
    B. slavery
    *C. patrimonialism
    D. feudalism
    E. primitive communism

11. An important part of what Marx called "surplus value" is
*A. profit   D. inflation
 B. exchange-value   E. capital
 C. use-value

12. The capitalists are temporarily able to squeeze the workers more and more
    because of what Marx called the
     A. lumpen-proletariat
    *B. industrial reserve army
     C. underclass
     D. imperialism
     E. socially-attached intelligentsia

13. What ultimately leads to the classless society is the abolition of
     A. the state   *D. private property
     B. poverty   E. the division of labor
     C. slavery

14. Questioning Marx's belief in the spontaneity of revolution, Lenin saw the
    proletariat developing mere
     A. counterrevolution   D. capitalist relationships
     B. idiocy of rural life   E. polarization of wealth
    *C. trade union consciousness

15. The Leninist party was to serve as the
     A. substitute for the state
    *B. vanguard of the proletariat
     C. home for all the masses
     D. dictatorship of the proletariat
     E. Third International

16. Lenin's formula for combining freedom and discipline in the party was
    called
     A. the leadership principle   D. the cult of personality
     B. devolution of authority   *E. democratic centralism
     C. left-wing communism

17. Stalin's contribution to modern communist ideology came mainly in the
    areas of
    *A. nationalism and the state   D. materialism and idealism
     B. the party and the masses   E. economics and politics
     C. proletariat and peasantry

18. Mao Tse-tung's movement away from strict economic determinism reflects
    *A. voluntarism   D. fatalism
     B. nationalism   E. pragmatism
     C. idealism

19. More than any previous communist theorist, Mao Tse-tung seemed to favor
     A. the intelligentsia   D. the petty bourgeoisie
     B. the national bourgeoisie   E. the bureaucracy
    *C. the peasants

20. Eduard Bernstein, an early social democrat, harshly criticized what he

74

called the theory of

A. dialectic   D. incrementalism
B. socialism   E. capitalism
*C. catastrophe

21. The bone of contention between left-wing and moderate social democrats
seems to be

A. revolution   D. the peasantry
B. violence   E. nationalism
*C. the welfare state

22. In general philosophy, modern-day Christian Democracy hails back most
clearly to

A. Sir Thomas More   D. Tomasso Campanella
*B. St. Thomas Aquinas   E. St. Augustine
C. Pope Pius IX

23. A primary source of classic liberal thought is

A. Edmund Burke   D. Karl Marx
B. John Dewey   E. Jean-Jacques Rousseau
*C. John Locke

24. Anticlericalism most closely suggests

A. irreligion   D. agnosticism
B. atheism   *E. mistrust of church activities
C. caesaro-papism

25. Edmund Burke went beyond the classic liberal notion of social contract
because he advocated a more

A. individualistic theory   D. anarchistic theory
*B. organic theory   E. pessimistic theory
C. atomistic theory

26. Instead of a democratic political order Edmund Burke favored rule by a

*A. natural aristocracy   D. managerial elite
B. heredity nobility   E. caste system
C. mass democracy

27. Poujadism appeals strongly to

A. the extremely rich   D. the bureaucracy
B. the working class   *E. the petty bourgeoisie
C. the managerial elite

28. The Fascist defense of the charismatic leader makes much of his so-called

*A. intuition   D. percipience
B. divinity   E. common sense
C. intelligence

29. Who can be called the "father" of modern racist ideology?

A. Burke   D. Darwin
B. De Maistre   E. Chamberlain
*C. Gobineau

30. A salient difference between the ideologies of Hitler and Mussolini

involves the importance of the

A. proletariat   D. social classes
B. church   E. leader
*C. state

Completion Questions

1. In economics, most anarchists favor <u>SOCIALISM</u>.

2. Marx sometimes called his doctrine <u>SCIENTIFIC</u> socialism.

3. While Marx was a materialist, his predecessor Hegel was a(n) <u>IDEALIST</u>.

4. The third step in a dialectical process is the <u>SYNTHESIS</u>.

5. Another Marxist name for the class of capitalists is the <u>BOURGEOISIE</u>.

6. Lenin saw in <u>IMPERIALISM</u> something of a Trojan horse of capitalism in its highest stage.

7. In 1925 Stalin defined <u>SOCIALISM</u> as the "transformation from a society with the dictatorship of the proletariat to a stateless society."

8. When Mao warned artists never to lose touch with the masses, this reflected his <u>POPULISM</u>.

9. The social democrat Crosland suggested that the traditional socialist concern with the problem of <u>OWNERSHIP</u> was increasingly irrelevant to social and economic realities.

10. G. D. H. Cole criticized moderate social democrats who preferred the "<u>OPEN</u>" society to the traditional socialist goal of the "classless" society.

11. The fountainhead of Christian Democratic doctrines is the notion of <u>NATURAL</u> law.

12. Early liberal thinkers entertained the notion of a social <u>CONTRACT</u>.

13. Early liberal thinkers were suspicious of <u>DEMOCRACY</u>.

14. While rejecting equality of condition, liberalism historically has favored equality of <u>OPPORTUNITY</u>.

15. John Dewey charged that early schools of liberalism tended to confuse mere change with genuine <u>PROGRESS</u>.

16. As a conservative, the poet T. S. Eliot was a strong defender of the <u>ARISTOCRATIC</u> principle.

17. Because of their doubts about the goodness of human nature, conservatives can be called social PESSIMISTS.

18. As opposed to metropolitan centers, poujadism defends the PERIPHERY.

19. The Social CREDIT movement in Canada has many poujadist elements.

20. According to Fascist ideology, "the STATE is absolute, individuals and groups relative."

21. It was apparently from Pareto that Italian Fascism borrowed its stress on ELITES.

22. Fascism's preoccupation with Roman-style imperialism helps explain the Italian conquest of ETHIOPIA in 1935.

23. Somewhat akin to later communist ideas, Fascism's preoccupation with will power and activism can be called VOLUNTARISM.

24. Fascism's anti-Marxism comes out in Mussolini's repudiation of the doctrine of historical MATERIALISM.

25. Fascist CORPORATIVISM was advanced as an alternative to liberal capitalism on the one hand and communism on the other.

26. Racism in the narrow sense involves a philosophy of HISTORY concerned with race and culture.

27. For Count Gobineau the ARYAN branch of the white race gave the impulse to most civilizations.

28. Houston Stewart Chamberlain saw modern history as a titanic struggle between the Teutonic peoples and the JEWS.

29. Hitler saw various races as either culture creators, culture bearers, or culture DESTROYERS.

30. A. James Gregor argues that originally Fascist themes pervade all modern RADICAL ideologies.

True-False Questions

1. Anarchists admit that the modern democratic state is a considerable improvement over its absolutist predecessor. (F)

2. The relationship between the substructure and the superstructure could exemplify a Marxist contradiction. (T)

3. If we concentrate on long-term goals rather than short-term means, Karl Marx was as much of a "utopian socialist" as some of those he criticized by that term. (T)

4. The progression Marx, Lenin, Stalin, Mao represents an increasingly deterministic strain in communist ideology. (F)

5. Modern social democrats would seem to follow C. A. R. Crosland's suggestion that the heart of socialism lies more in morality than in economics. (T)

6. The welfare state is simply another name for socialism. (F)

7. Because of religious principles Christian Democracy is even more individualistic than classical liberalism. (F)

8. Modern liberalism has a friendlier attitude to both the state and the masses than did classic liberalism. (T)

9. Liberalism preaches reform rather than revolution or reaction. (T)

10. Conservatism is the only point on the ideological spectrum that features an organic approach to both state and society. (F)

11. Conservatism is simply the desire to preserve the status quo. (F)

12. The xenophobia of poujadism reminds one of the hypernationalism of Fascism. (T)

13. Fascist voluntarism stresses the leader and the elite, while communist voluntarism (at least in theory) stresses the party and the masses. (T)

14. The racism of Gobineau, Chamberlain, and Hitler stress the absolute superiority of the Aryans. (F)

15. It becomes more difficult to employ the terms left and right with precision the longer the timespan we have before us. (T)

NOTES